"*FALLING* IS BEAUTIFULLY WRITTEN AND DISARMING IN ITS HONESTY...

Taylor's memoir is more than the story of a divorce, it is the story of his dawning maturity, insight, and morality."

—*Rocky Mountain News*

"It is a testament to the unsparing fullness of the book that the reader comes away not only with a sense of the 'grim satisfactions of duty' in this marriage but also with an acute portrait of two people living in a painful kind of stasis . . . To honestly capture, as *Falling* does, the paradoxical condition in which romantic love between people may wither and die even as the emotional bonds and dependencies between them continue to strengthen is to illuminate the tragic nature of human ambivalence . . . It is this hard truth that shines out from the heart of this sad, brave book."

—*Vogue*

"Aside from the effortless precision of his prose and his male perspective, it's Taylor's tone that distinguishes his story. Sadness, not bitterness, fills the book . . . Taylor feels a deep sense of loss—both for his family and for the part of himself that was defined by his family."

—*Kirkus Reviews*

"Fascinating . . . Compellingly honest . . . A very thought-provoking study of one man's life and love . . . What Taylor learns about marriage and divorce through his own experiences is written about extremely thoughtfully."

—*Gulf Coast Woman*

"Remarkable . . . Haunting . . . Within a chapter, he had me gripped."

—*The Times* (London)

falling

Also by John Taylor

STORMING THE MAGIC KINGDOM

CIRCUS OF AMBITION

JOHN TAYLOR

falling

the story of one marriage

BALLANTINE BOOKS • NEW YORK

A Ballantine Book
Published by The Ballantine Publishing Group
Copyright © 1999 John Taylor

Brief portions of this work originally appeared in a different
form in *Esquire* magazine.

www.randomhouse.com/BB/

Library of Congress Catalog Card Number: 00-104672

ISBN 0-345-43956-2

This is edition is published by arrangement with Random
House, Inc.

Manufactured in the United States of America

First Trade Paperback Edition: August 2000

10 9 8 7 6 5 4 3 2 1

author's note

Although this is a work of nonfiction, I have changed the names and some of the identifying details of many of the people I have written about, including Alexandra Carras, Jill Hartmann, and Sheryl Gates. I have also taken the liberty of transposing a few minor scenes and situations. My objective with these alterations was not to novelize the facts for the sake of artificial drama but to produce a coherent narrative that honored privacy while authentically reflecting events, experiences, and emotions.

For you, Jess,
I'll always be there

We thought we had tied the knot of our marriages more firmly by removing all means of dissolving them; but the bond of hearts and affections has become more loose and slack as that of constraint has been drawn closer. And, on the other hand, what made marriages to be so long honoured and so secure in Rome was the liberty to break them off at will. They loved their wives the better as long as there was the chance of losing them and, with full liberty of divorce, five hundred years and more passed by before any took advantage of it.

Michel de Montaigne

one

Chapter 1

"We have to separate," my wife told me. It was a late-summer evening eleven and a half years after we had gotten married. We were on our deck, drinking gin-and-tonics and smoking cigarettes, an entitlement of marital stress. The setting sun cast rose-colored shadows across the mansard roof of the Victorian elementary school visible beyond the hickory tree in our next-door neighbor's backyard. A straggling bumblebee drowsed in the pots of geraniums that, together with the wooden boxes of clematis and petunias and ivy, lined the deck's warping plank floor. A light breeze out of the east enhanced the quiet by sweeping the noise of the city traffic seaward. The elementary school had an outdoor basketball court, where sometimes after work I would take my daughter to practice her pitching, and the noise from a game—preadolescent shouts, the tripping thump of the dribbled ball and its rattled smack against the metal backboard—drifted across the intervening gardens.

"We do?" I asked. After all, our marriage wasn't hellish, it was simply dispiriting. My wife and I didn't hate each other, we simply got on each other's nerves. Over the years we each had accumulated a store of minor unresolved grievances. Our marriage was a mechanism so encrusted with small disappointments and petty grudges that its parts no longer closed.

My wife exhaled impatiently—she was English and had that hurried European way of smoking—and tapped her cigarette into a flowerpot.

"What about the money?" I asked.

In the three years during which we had struggled toward, floundered against, and pulled back from the idea of separating, I had played the accountant. I was bad at math—I disliked even the minor computation involved in paying bills, usually postponing the chore for so long that late fees appeared on the following month's statements—but I had sat down and figured out the cost of supporting two households, the tax disadvantages of filing separately, what I made, what I'd need, and what my wife and our daughter would need. Twenty years after finishing college, I was finally earning a decent though hardly spectacular salary. If we separated, I'd again end up living like an undergraduate. I saw the life quite clearly: a shabby railroad apartment, bookcases made from milk crates, fried-egg sandwiches, a portable black-and-white TV with tinfoil wrapped around the antenna. My wife's situation would be just as grim, and probably, in the long run, even worse. She had no job. She had come down with Parkinson's disease shortly after our daughter was born and her medical condition would make it difficult for her to find work now. What was she supposed to do? How would she support herself in the years ahead?

"We can't stay together just for the money," my wife said.

I thought about the phrase "an irretrievable breakdown of the marriage." There is something deceptive about it. The passive, impersonal structure, the dry legalities of the language, conceal a lie. It suggests that a marriage has an independent organic existence. It exonerates us by portraying us as merely the clinicians pronouncing the body dead.

But at what precise point does the breakdown of a marriage become irretrievable? The moment we declare it so, and no sooner. And the marriage doesn't just break down. We disconnect the life support. While it requires will to make a marriage work, it also requires a horrifying act of will to bring one to an end.

My wife put out her cigarette and looked at me. There was nothing insistent or demanding in her eyes, the pale gray-green eyes of her Russian grandparents. She was, I realized, making an appeal to me. We had to help each other bring it to an end. I felt, at that moment, an exaltingly pure sense of complicity and understanding. To summon the strength to proceed we would need to reassure each other, to depend on and trust each other. We would have to work together to dissolve the marriage in a way we had never been able to do to sustain it. I saw all this with piercing clarity, and then I thought, But if we are capable of such a delicate and complicated collaboration, maybe we should stay together after all.

My wife and I were falling through the darkness. We had been for years. Our impending separation rushed toward us, but spinning in the black air, unable to see, we had no idea when the moment of impact would actually arrive.

During that time the national debate over divorce had grown louder and, I felt, increasingly fatuous. Getting divorced had come to be regarded as an act of cowardice, a failure of character, an abdication of responsibility. Even liberals, who in the seventies had been the proponents of divorce reform, began to consider it a display of intellectual independence to attack the "divorce epidemic," as it was invariably called. They connected the existence of the epidemic to the supposedly pernicious spread of "moral relativism." Instead of faithfully adhering to codes—of duty, honor, family—they complained, people nowadays continually improvised their ethics to justify the indulgence of their desires.

At its worst, this charge reeked to me of self-righteousness, of false piety, and at times of religious intimidation. It was the rehearsed indignation of professional moralists who had discovered a market for sanctimonious rhetoric. But even at its most sincere, it simply seemed oblivious to lived experience. No one I knew who had decided to divorce undertook it lightly. It was a wrenching decision, fraught with remorse and heartache, imperiled by moments of genuine terror, and it had almost invariably been postponed for years. Who had the right, I wanted to know, to moralize about these choices, to add the weight of public censure to the private anguish they already entailed?

Most of the couples I knew who had gotten divorced, particularly those with children, seemed irreparably altered. Defeat haunted them. Their futures had been sapped of meaning. Other couples treated them gingerly, like convalescing soldiers, but also with caution, as if their misfortune might be contagious.

As the social debate intensified, and as my wife and I continued our discussions about separating, divorce had begun to ravage our neighborhood. It struck like some form of natural disaster, leveling one house while leaving the next intact. Our daughter's nursery school teacher, a vivacious woman with dark eyes and plump legs, was the first person my wife and I knew, the first of our age, to get divorced; she and her husband, she later explained to my wife, simply didn't get along. One day our daughter came home to tell us that the teacher, while leading the class in song, had burst into tears. I expected my daughter to ask us why, but children are much more comfortable with life's inexplicabilities; she said nothing.

An actor and a legal clerk, the parents of one of our daughter's schoolmates, split up next. So did an editor and a publicist known for their nightmarishly relentless quarreling. Then a neighbor, a software programmer and passionate libertarian, left his wife; their son's misbehavior became compulsive and he was thrown out of school. The architect and the former advertising agent we had become friends with, the accountant and the school psychologist whose son pestered our daughter in the preschool they both attended, the police detective and the physical therapist in the squat limestone at the end of the block—they all separated.

As time passed, the breakups became increasingly spectacular and baroque. The longer the marriage, the more deranged the couple seemed to have become. One man, afraid to confront his domineering wife, moved out with no prior warning and lived in his office for the next four years. Another man, whom I had met when we brought our wives to the same Lamaze class years ago, moved into the basement of his house when his wife refused to go off Prozac. It cost them one thousand dollars in legal fees just to decide what type of door would separate the basement from the main house.

I ran into a man on the subway whose daughter played on my daughter's baseball team. I had seen him at games, a slight fellow with sad watery eyes and a gray mustache yellowing at the corners of his mouth. He was divorced, he said. His wife had become a lesbian. She used to beat him, he said, but she had acquired sole custody of their daughter by falsely claiming he had beaten her. Although she had moved in with another woman, and although the only time he could see his daughter was at the baseball games, the courts required him to pay both child support and maintenance. I looked at him speechlessly. He shrugged and, as the train pulled into his station, touched me on the shoulder and said, "See you at the game."

These stories belied the notion that, as the social conservatives and their liberal allies liked to maintain, divorce had become a casual, guilt-free enterprise pursued by the irresponsible with the encouragement of a licentious society. They frightened me.

But the stories also aroused a voyeuristic excitement. It was not simply the display of psychic wounds, the blood and pain of lives in collision, that attracted me. I wanted to know how they all knew when they had reached an irretrievable breakdown. How did they know they had arrived? I sought the points of demarcation.

Chapter 2

Over the years, when women asked me in vexed, slightly irritated voices why my wife and I did get married, the only explanation I could offer was, "It seemed like a good idea at the time."

My response sounded halting and apologetic, as if, looking back, my own behavior bewildered me. But marriage, at the time I got married, *did* seem like a good idea. Not that I gave it much thought. I was twenty-eight and utterly unaware of the course my life might take. I had no idea of the consolations and confinements marriage offered. I never thought to ask myself what type of woman—compliant, independent, provocative, driven, nurturing, passionate—would be best for me. Who does? The question can only be answered in retrospect. Marriage, I came to believe at the time I was trying to figure out why mine was falling apart, is largely a matter of luck.

My parents' marriage proved that.

My parents met in 1954 at the Cafe du Monde, a coffee shop just off Bourbon Street in New Orleans. It was a random encounter, one that could have easily failed to take place, but then it is always the subsequent developments that retroactively invest the chance event with the aura of predestination. My father was twenty-two, a flight cadet at the Pensacola naval air station. My mother, nineteen, was studying nursing at Tulane. Each of my parents had gone to the Cafe du Monde with a group of friends. The two groups, one of slim naval aviators in khaki uniforms, the other of bright-eyed young women with bobbed hair and pleated skirts, sat at separate tables, sipping their coffee and smoking, aware of but not acknowledging one another's presence until a photographer approached the men and offered to take their picture, at which point my father asked the women if they would pose with them, "so our mothers will think we have girlfriends." The women agreed, and afterward they all sat together talking awkwardly until one of the women realized she had attended my father's brother's wedding the previous year in Montgomery. The establishment of this social connection reassured the women, and my father was able to ask my mother for a date.

During the next two months, my father drove into New Orleans to see my mother six or seven times. Then he was assigned to the air station in Cherry Point, North Carolina. From there he wrote to her, proposing. She took the train up and they were married five months after they met. Immediately after the wedding, my father was shipped off to Japan and my mother blithely followed. In our family mythology, the brevity of the courtship underscored the inevitability of the union. My parents were meant for each other, fated even. They recognized this immediately and moved to join their lives together. But to me, today, their behavior seems rash, impulsive, immature, an act of outright folly. They had known each other for two months. During that time they had lived some two hundred miles apart and had seen each other only on weekends. They were virtual strangers! And one was a teenager!

What could they possibly have known about each other at that point? What could they have known about themselves? Neither of them—the nineteen-year-old bride, the twenty-two-year-old husband—had the slightest idea what awaited them in life, how they'd react to it, and what they would need from the person they married.

If my daughter, when she turns nineteen, calls me and announces she's going to marry a twenty-one-year-old soldier she met six weeks ago, I'll be mortified. I'll refuse to let her throw her life away so impulsively. I might even, if I thought it would work, lock her in the cellar. And, in fact, when my youngest sister, at that same age, declared she was marrying a graduate student in mathematics who was a born-again Christian, my entire family was aghast, and not over the question of religion. Cynthia, we all agreed, was simply too young, too unformed, too unsure of herself, to make such a commitment. We didn't lock her in the cellar, but before we eventually talked her out of the marriage, some equivalent possibility did get discussed.

And yet my parents' marriage has been stable and productive and the family they raised a happy one—though two years before I got married a psychologist spent nine months trying to convince me that this was a delusion. If their success was due to luck, then how did my parents get so lucky?

My mother was born and raised in Lone Mountain, Tennessee, a remote Appalachian village thirty miles south of Cumberland Gap. The region is beautiful but unyielding. In the early morning, fog languishes in ethereal drifts in the hollows and along the time-softened ridges, but many of the hillsides are too steep to farm, and in the valleys where the ground is sufficiently flat the underlying shale often pushes through the shallow, flinty soil. Even today, many of the people who live there don't work full-time; they scrape by on their tobacco allotment, on fishing and hunting and odd jobs.

My mother's father was Cawood Rose, a mechanic who

owned an automobile repair shop in Tazewell, the county seat, eight miles north of Lone Mountain. When my mother was five, Cawood became embroiled in a feud with two brothers, Hadad and Shultzy Robinson, who owned a café two doors down from the garage. According to family legend, Shultzy was involved in a stolen-car ring, and when Cawood found out about it, Shultzy became afraid my grandfather might turn him in and began threatening him. One night in 1940, Cawood, who was twenty-eight at the time, was drinking in the Midway Tavern with a tobacco buyer when Shultzy came through the door with a drawn pistol. In the shoot-out that erupted, Shultzy missed my grandfather, who ducked behind a beer cooler, but accidentally shot and killed the tobacco buyer before my grandfather, who was carrying a revolver, killed him. Although the killing was ruled self-defense, Shultzy's brother Hadad pledged to seek revenge, and for five weeks Cawood moved his young family to Kingsport. Eventually he decided, as his wife, my grandmother Sally, would later explain, "he couldn't keep running forever," and he returned to Tazewell. A couple of days later he was in his garage, which was across the street from the courthouse, working under the hood of a long-haul truck when Hadad walked up behind him with a shotgun and emptied both barrels into his back. He died on the garage floor.

My grandmother moved with her two children back to her parents' house. My great-grandfather, Byrd Payne, ran the Lone Mountain general store along with his brother, Fate. Byrd and his wife, Sallie A., had ten children, the youngest of whom was only a few years older than my mother, and they all lived in a white frame house with a tin roof and a cement porch on a dirt road running parallel to the railroad tracks that wound down from Middlesboro to Knoxville. Since my grandmother began working six days a week as a dental assistant in Tazewell, my mother was raised primarily by her uncles, who served as surrogate fathers, and her grandmother, a teetotaling southern Baptist with a strict code of justice; she would make my mother select the branch from the willow tree when she decided my mother's misbehavior warranted a whipping. When my mother was thirteen, her mother, thinking it best, sent her to live with an aunt in Kansas City.

And so, although she was part of an extended mountain family, my mother grew up haunted by the death of her father and with the sense that her circumstances were precarious. Dependent on the forbearance of relatives, she developed a fear of imposing on others and a deep longing for a place of her own. The man she married turned out to be ceaselessly restless; we never lived in a place without the knowledge that we would leave it in a year or two. And so my mother satisfied her desire for belonging in our family. She claimed it, idealized it, invested everything she had in it. The family was where she made her stand.

If my mother was, in a sense, seeking a family, my father was, in a somewhat different sense, fleeing one. My father had grown up in Nashville. His father lost a small fortune in the Depression and never recovered. When I knew him, he had a job as an insurance adjuster—work that suggested to me both an eminent respectability and a tedium so extreme it was almost mystical. He was a quiet, remote man; he dressed fastidiously, smoked menthol cigarettes, and always wore a hat. His wife, my grandmother, had by far the stronger personality. She was intelligent, domineering, and slightly hysterical. Her father had died when she was young, and when her mother remarried, her stepfather refused to let her keep a picture of her real father in the house. Suppressing emotion had become for her a survival strategy. She learned as a child to live life below the surface.

If she had been born fifty years later, she might have become a litigator, or a hedge-fund manager, or a lobbyist. As it was, the only arena for the exercise of her will was the family's small two-bedroom house on Kenner Avenue, near Bellemeade. It vibrated with her frustrated aspirations. Every surface gleamed. Her two sons were forbidden to play in the parlor, with its striped horse-hair couch and cherrywood writing table and glass-enclosed book-case containing Carl Sandburg's six-volume biography of Lincoln. They left the house each morning with wet, perfectly combed hair; they used a manual lawn mower, with scissoring parabolic blades, to keep the small, steeply angled lawn in perfect trim. It was a tense household—the quiet, mild father, the exacting, thwarted mother—and my father was eager to flee it. He finished high school at sixteen, graduated from Vanderbilt, and then, with the Korean War under way, enlisted in the navy with the intention, when he got out, of joining the foreign service and living abroad in distant capitals with exotic names like Jakarta and Khartoum, steaming, tumultuous cities far from Nashville.

My sense of myself as a lucky person originated with my family. I am one of the few people I know who admit to having come from a happy family. I feel at times that this is an oddity, and not just un-conventional and eccentric but suspect, as if the happy family is a contradiction in terms, a psychological oxymoron.

Every family has its own mythology: in one the father is King Lear, in another the eldest son is Icarus, in a third the mother is Medea. At the end of the twentieth century most of that mythol-ogy centers on betrayal, violation, antagonism, pain, the inheri-tance of dysfunction. People of my generation, even those who have become parents themselves, seem unable to forgive *their* par-ents for being merely human. They take a perverse pride in de-nouncing their families. I find their bitterness difficult to comprehend. Why are they so uncharitable, so devoid of compas-sion? Why have they failed to understand, or refuse to accept, that their parents are merely human beings like themselves, fallible, prone to misjudgment, but largely well-intentioned?

Our family had its mythology as well. But it wasn't structured around dysfunction. The central theme in our mythology was that we were the chosen. We were the elect, the favored. We were golden.

I decided early on I wanted to be a father like my father, and it is an ambition that, even though I have felt I never realized it, I never abandoned. My father, when I was growing up, was a rationalist: patient, even-tempered, generous, firm. He believed that life was fragile, but not tragic. He believed in freedom rather than tradition, choice rather than fate, the triumph of hope over experience. He believed that principle formed the core of character and that morality was essentially spiritual. It existed, in his view, not simply as a behavioral mechanism, a learned response to reward and punishment, but as a means of maintaining internal equilibrium. He never cheated on his taxes or padded his expense account. He taught by example. He considered self-promotion to be improper, believing that in an essentially moral universe—and to him history represented the triumph of morality—hard work would in the end be rewarded. He refused to play politics to compromise his convictions for personal gain, and when, as a result he reached the penultimate but not the highest rung in his profession, I considered that to be, in its own way, a greater achievement.

While my parents were young, very young, when they got married, they never acted childishly. They embraced responsibility. Indeed, they behaved with such maturity and poise that it's hard for me to grasp how young they were. My mother and father had set out to create the sort of family they had been denied. Both of them believed in the possibility of family, both had been prepared by their own childhoods to work toward it. The constraints of fidelity, the burdens of parenthood, the challenges of intimacy— none of these seemed to require sacrifice or even much effort on their part. It's tempting to say they were also temperamentally suited for their roles, but the fact is that marriage did not just provide them with roles. It did much more. It allowed them to realize themselves, to be who they were.

My mother, who was always driving one of us somewhere, wore scarves, sunglasses, and ruby-red lipstick. My father wrote Kiplingesque poems, which he recited to us on our birthdays, and occasionally smoked a pipe. My mother was raised a Baptist, my father a Methodist, but after they married they chose to become Unitarians. Both had come from families ruled by tempestuous emotion, and Unitarianism embodied the cool, enlightened secularism that was their adopted style. They believed in self-control. They rarely argued, and almost never in front of the children. They spanked me reluctantly and my sisters not at all. They were consistent but not excessive in their praise. We were, as a family, young, flexible, and contemporary. We radiated confidence. We were always on the move. We were golden.

Chapter 3

"We never should have gotten married," *my wife told me any number* of times over the years. Sometimes she would say this with exasperation, sometimes in despair. She could make it an accusation, hurled at me, or a bitter refrain, murmured to herself, or a simple statement of fact, delivered with quiet, almost philosophical resignation.

She felt imprisoned by the choice she'd made, as if she'd taken a wrong turn onto a road from which there are no exits. It seemed to her such a glaringly obvious mistake that, she thought, we were fools not to have recognized it at the time. "We were fools," she would say. "Fools."

I felt differently. It *had* seemed like a good idea at the time, I would tell Maureen. Maybe it even *was* a good idea at the time. It just hadn't worked out the way we'd intended.

But, I realized later, that was not quite accurate. The problem was that we were never clear, either to each other or to ourselves, what our true intentions were.

I was not, at the time I met Maureen, looking for a wife. Not because, like a number of the men I knew, I instinctively feared commitment, or loved my solitude, or wanted to hang with the guys. I did assume I'd get married one day and have a large, boisterous family and live in a rambling, even slightly shabby house, but that was down the road. Somewhere down the road. It would happen when I met the girl from Philadelphia.

I can remember, when I was about ten, asking my mother whom I was going to marry. "One day you'll meet a girl from Philadelphia," she said, "and you'll look at her and you'll know she's the one." I don't know why she chose Philadelphia. It could have been any city, and even at age ten I knew she didn't of course mean the girl would literally come from Philadelphia. Still, that phrase—"the girl from Philadelphia"—had an undeniable ring. The mellifluous and historic name suggested to me a slender young woman of unspecified beauty whose quiet breeding concealed a passionate nature. Ever since, I had kept my eye out for the girl from Philadelphia. I hadn't found her yet, but I knew she was out there. The girl who was meant for me.

I was twenty-six at the time I met Maureen. My experiences with women were typical for someone of my age and generation. I could remember the names of all but one of the women I had slept with—and her name is the only thing about her that I can't recall. I had fallen in love with four of them and for two years had lived with one of the four, Barbara, the daughter of a New England country lawyer.

I liked women. I had grown up an only son, with three younger sisters, and I was never happier than when I was surrounded by women. They were, I've always felt, more interesting than men. The status-jockeying, the relentless competitive ribbing, and the passionate discussions of sports and women's bodies that were the essence of male society bored and irritated me, made me feel incompetent. Men were rigidly external. Women led rich interior lives. They were empathic and alert and psychologically complex. Their desire for emotional connection made them more engaged, more sensitive to truth, more inquiring, and provided them with a spiritual intentionality that men lacked. Women, for all the talk of the self-esteem problems that supposedly afflict their gender, always seemed to me more poised and resourceful than men. Since, for the most part, they did not have the option of resorting to violence, they had evolved more sophisticated strategies for dealing with the unexpected.

When I was in the sixth grade I developed an infatuation for a girl named Christine Bebb. She had blond hair that fell over her blue eyes and a slightly plump chin. Since she was in another class, I had hardly ever spoken to her, but distance intensifies infatuation, and one Saturday I rode my bicycle three miles to a drugstore where, from inside a wooden phone booth, I called her house. My hands were damp. I hung up before the phone rang, rehearsed my lines, called again. Christine answered.

"Hi, it's John Taylor," I said. "Do you want to go steady?"

"John, my folks have some people over right now," she said. "Can I call you back?"

"Sure."

I hung up and rode home. I actually expected her to return my call and spent the weekend hanging around the house waiting for the phone to ring. It never did, and when I got to school on Monday I found out she had told all her friends, who had told the entire sixth grade, what had happened. The mortification I felt is not what I remember most vividly. It is instead her extraordinary composure in the face of my unexpected and ridiculous call. She hadn't paused. Where had she come up with such a shrewd pretext for evading my offer? How had she managed to deliver it so effortlessly?

Two years later, in another school in another country, I was infatuated with another girl named Christine. Again I was clueless about how to pursue her. One day as we walked toward the cafeteria I lunged for her hand, but in my clumsiness I dropped a book

I was carrying. I stopped to pick it up, and when I turned back to her she had shifted her books to the arm nearest me and was holding them against her chest, which meant that her hand, the hand I had tried to clutch, had suddenly become unavailable. We walked along, continuing our conversation, as if nothing had happened. The move was so adroit, it was such a perfect solution to the awkwardness of the situation, that even today it seems to me remarkable. Who were these girls? How did they acquire such composure and ingenuity?

Two years after that, I was smoking cigarettes on a wooded hilltop with another girl. She was fifteen, I was sixteen.

"Do you know what it means when someone blows smoke in your face?" she asked.

"No."

"It means they want to make love," she said and coolly expelled a cloud of smoke in my direction.

Women knew what they wanted and what they didn't want, it always seemed to me, and they knew how to go after the former and avoid the latter. They knew how to handle themselves.

Since moving to New York I had taken up with a number of women: an aspiring actress who, along with her roommate, chanted Buddhist prayers for half an hour every night while I read in the bedroom; a manager with AT&T who stunned me by confessing after we had gone to bed together that she had been a virgin but had felt too awkward about it to tell me beforehand; an opinionated young teacher from a wealthy Chicago family; another teacher, eight years older than I was, who belonged to a female support group with the acronym WINGS, for Women In New Growth Situations; a blond banker with a mannish gait; a coffee-colored woman whose family was from Jamaica and who brought every conversation around to race; a reed-thin Barnard student with a hoarse laugh and political ambitions; a tense, feverish copy editor who gave me a volume of Howard Nemerov's poems; an Italian American girl from Brooklyn, the daughter of a police detective, who had never once ventured north of the Whitestone Bridge. These were all fascinating women, mysterious and compelling in certain ways, alarming in others, but none of them was the girl from Philadelphia.

I met my wife through Robin, a friend who worked in the administrative department of the magazine that then employed me. One spring day around noon I dropped by Robin's office—a windowless room, like mine, down a gray carpeted hallway—and Maureen was there, sitting in the modular plastic visitor's chair Robin kept in front of her desk. I knocked on the open door. Maureen swiveled around. She was slight, with curling sun-streaked hair. It was hard to tell how old she was. She had an unlined, ageless face, an actress's face. Her white tennis shoes, worn without socks, and her green cotton jumpsuit, and the way she had set her ponytail off-center, behind one ear, all made her seem young and slightly raffish. She spoke in a quiet, gracious, somewhat cool tone. Her accent was more Continental than English, with gentle, rounded cadences. ("You're British?" exclaimed a real estate agent who was showing us an apartment shortly before our wedding. "I thought you were just cultured.") I thought she was French.

I was immediately taken with her. I had recently stopped seeing the Italian American daughter of the vice cop, and I persuaded Robin to give me Maureen's number. When I called Maureen, she seemed mystified. She later said she thought I was going to offer her work. What that meant, though I didn't realize it at the time, was that she was more aware of our age difference than I was, that when she had swiveled around as I entered Robin's office the day we met a sense of possibility had not immediately ignited inside her the way it had in me. Even so, she agreed to meet me for dinner.

I took her to an inexpensive French restaurant I knew, a narrow place, hot, crowded, and smoky back in the days when people were still allowed to smoke in restaurants. Brusque Norman women in blue aprons served customers at tiny tables jammed along the wall. When Maureen ordered mussels, I was intrigued. It would never have occurred to me to order mussels. I rarely even ordered fish. The choice of mussels bespoke not just a sophisticated European palate but an entire range of cultural references that I, a twenty-six-year-old American, was only dimly aware of.

Maureen told me she had been raised in London, had attended the Sorbonne for a couple of years, returned to London, where she worked for different British newspapers before moving first to Israel, then Hong Kong, and eventually ending up back in Paris. She'd gotten a job at the *International Herald Tribune* but felt curious about New York. She had visited the city on a vacation and fallen in love with it, had flown back to Paris, quit her job, packed her things, and returned to New York, moving, with only a few clothes, limited funds, and a short list of contacts, into the Barbizon hotel.

"I told myself I'd try it for a year," she said.

Her sense of adventure—this spontaneous, free-spirited, heedless approach to life—dazzled me. Such willingness to pursue an impulse made almost everyone else I knew seem drab. It made *me* seem that way, a cautious and conventional young man hedging my real potential against the opportunities for advancement in the company where I worked and where I felt, like all young men in entry-level positions, grossly unappreciated. Where did Maureen, where did anyone, but particularly where did a woman so quiet and self-contained get that sort of daring?

"How many more months do you have left?" I asked.

"Four."

"Are you going to go back?"

"I don't know," she said. "I'm rather enjoying it here."

Chapter 4

S hortly after I was born, my father joined the foreign service, and while I was growing up my family moved more than a dozen times. Over the years we lived in Japan, California, Ghana, Virginia, Taiwan, Michigan, Borneo, Hong Kong, Maryland, and South Africa. One of my most vivid memories about each of these places was our taking leave of it, the moment when, as we drove off, I would turn in my seat for a last look through the rear window. My mother would say, "Good-bye, Prosperity Avenue," or "Good-bye, Blue Gate," or "Good-bye, Wells Street," and my father would say, "Off we go on a wonderful new adventure," and my sisters would giggle excitedly. As I looked back I would think, *Never again,* and feel a profound pull, as if the place was reaching out, calling us back, begging us not to consign it to the past, trying to make us understand that we were leaving behind not just a house and a neighborhood but a large and irretrievable part of our lives.

I was born in Japan but we moved before I was one, and my earliest memories are of Ghana, where our next-door neighbor kept a pet monkey that periodically broke into our house and swung shrieking from the drapes and where the man across the street owned an ostrich he would ride after slipping a leather hood fitted with reins over its head. We left Ghana when I was four and, after a year in Washington, D.C., moved to Taichung, a small city on the island of Taiwan. There, we lived in a formal Japanese-style house. Tatamis covered the floors and upon entering the vestibule we were required to take off our shoes. The interior walls were made of glazed rice-paper mounted on sliding wooden frames. As a five-year-old I found myself unable to resist the temptation to poke holes in them, but the cook knew who had done the damage when he discovered it, and he slapped my hands. There was a formal Chinese garden in the back. Mottled carp and goldfish swam, their silky fins rippling, in the large pond, which was covered with lily pads, crossed by tiny arched bridges, and bordered with dwarf pines. A high wall with a blue wooden gate surrounded the house, and across the dirt road in front of it was an open field pitted with deep, muddy puddles where Chinese boys my age brought water buffalo to bathe.

After two years in Taichung, we moved to Taipei and lived in a small rural compound surrounded by rice paddies. The compound was at the base of a hill known as the Hill of a Thousand Steps because a seemingly endless staircase led to a Buddhist temple on the peak. The hill was sacred. Paths wound through the woods on its steep slopes. In the roots at the bases of the large banyan trees, the Chinese placed urns filled with the bones of the dead, whom they buried in coffins for ten years and then unearthed and potted.

In Borneo we lived in a colonial house that had mahogany shutters instead of windows or screens. We ate most of our meals on a terrace with orchid plants and a thatched roof, and we kept as a pet an anteater, which lacked personality and spent most of its time rooting placidly in the banana grove behind the kitchen. In Hong Kong we lived in a Spanish villa that Japanese officers had occupied during World War II. It sat near the top of a cliff—an abandoned and snake-infested antiaircraft gun emplacement was hidden in the trees above—and looked out across the South China

Sea, where, in the early light, wooden junks with red sails and huge yellow eyes painted on their prows tacked in their heavy wallowing fashion out to the fishing grounds.

The magical qualities of these places accentuated the sense of loss when we left. But since we were always moving on to other places that, my father assured us, were even more magical, the sense of loss carried an undercurrent of anticipation, of excitement and even joy. For much of my life I found it thrilling to leave a place, or a person, to take that final look and then turn away, facing the road ahead. The moment of departure, that moment when you consign some part of your life to the past, was for me a moment of promise as well. I loved to say good-bye.

Chapter 5

Moving had one other effect on me. It made me wonder, *Is this my real life?* Whenever we arrived in a new city and I was taken to a new school—particularly if this happened in the middle of the year, the principal opening a door with a frosted-glass window and ushering me into a classroom where all the students turned to stare—I would ask myself: Is this what's supposed to be happening to me? Or is my real life somewhere else, back in the place we left, or the place before that, or in some city like Calcutta or Islamabad where my father was offered but turned down a post? Are there true friends out there I should have had, girls I was intended to love?

As an adult I was still beset by the feeling that I was not living in the city where I truly belonged, that the woman I was with was not the one destiny had marked for me.

So, at what point did I decide that Maureen was the woman I ought to marry? It's hard to say. It seemed less a conclusion I reached on a particular occasion than the result of a slow accretion of moments, sand shifted by a current, but if I had to pick a point I would say it occurred that night in New Hampshire when we followed the stranger in the black Cougar up into the mountains.

One date had led to a second and then a third. By August we were spending much of our time together. Maureen came with me on assignments to Maine and Atlantic City. I accompanied her on a business trip to Houston. She was writing for a Paris newspaper at the time and it regularly sent her off to Los Angeles or San Francisco or Lynchburg, Tennessee. With her heart-shaped face and small features and tumbling reddish-golden hair, she was irresistibly attractive. I enjoyed the fact that we were seen as a couple. At a crowded party around that time, given by a female psychologist, one of the many friends Maureen made so effortlessly in those days, I ended up talking to a striking, morbidly pale architect who twisted a tendril of her raven hair and studied me with shadow-encircled eyes.

"Are you with someone?" she asked.

"Yes."

"Who?"

I pointed out Maureen, who was talking in the midst of an animated circle, and felt a powerful proprietary thrill as the woman measured herself against Maureen and found herself coming up short.

Maureen was quiet and cultivated, unselfish and gentle. But she also had a dry, sarcastic wit and an air of self-containment that made her seem elusive. She lacked the highly developed intentionality that defined so many of the women I knew, that vivid, even urgent sense of what it was they truly desired.

"What do you want to *do* with your life?" I asked Maureen that summer.

She shrugged. "I'm not particularly ambitious."

The remark confused me. Ablaze with ambition myself, I couldn't comprehend how someone might not only lack it but actually dismiss it, might regard it as somehow beside the point. It would be years before I realized how uninteresting ambition truly is.

That October I suggested we drive up to Vermont to see the foliage. I had gone to a boarding school in Vermont, had hiked the northern sections of the Long Trail, and for the past few years had wanted to return in autumn. It was customary among people I knew to scorn Vermont—the picture-postcard prettiness of the covered bridges and high-steepled churches, the ecological earnestness of the escaped New Yorkers who opened overpriced restaurants with names like the Ravelled Sleeve and the Mill on the Floss in converted barns, the cloying, suffocating preciousness of it all—but I liked the place. I liked the gaudy leaves, the white Federal houses with their formal black shutters, the unreconstructed utopianism of the hippies, the ostentatiously discreet road signs, the cunning venality with which the locals exploited the tourists. Now I had a chance to show the state in all its shameless seasonal splendor to Maureen.

I rented a car and we took the Taconic Parkway out of the city and then cut over through the Housatonic Mountains to Route 7. It was a glorious day, bright, cloudless, the damp air fragrant with the smell of decaying wood. The road swung and dipped following the contours of the tree-massed hills. We passed dry lake beds and stands of pines and hardwoods. The sun slanted through the fluttering leaves. Gusts of wind swirled them in coils across our path.

As we proceeded through the Berkshires and into the foothills of the Green Mountains, the tobacco-brown and mud-orange colors of the oaks began to give way to the scarlet leaves of the maples and the yellows of birches. I hadn't been up Route 7 in years, and it was more crowded than I remembered. Farm stands lined the roads, their tables piled with pumpkins and cider, with plastic-wrapped baked goods and wreaths made from corn husks and squash gourds. Drivers impetuously pulled off the road to stop at these stands, creating abrupt moments of peril. Tour buses, their elderly passengers peering intently through the tinted windows, roared past. I turned on the radio. A local announcer was describing how the Northern Kingdom of Vermont was at peak color, the Rutland area at about 70 percent color, and the southern zone near Bennington at 50 percent color. Maureen found this use of statistics hilarious. It seemed, in its quantification and reductive-ness of beauty, quintessentially American, and we both laughed.

To get away from the traffic, I turned off onto a smaller road. We followed a turbulent black river through a narrow, chilly valley that abruptly widened into dairy pasture. Out in the middle of the open ground stood a single massive maple, fallen leaves forming a perfect bloodred circle on the grass under it. I found a county road and drove up into the mountains, then turned onto a dirt track that climbed steeply. I stopped the car and we walked into the forest, beneath the rustling canopy, until we came to a sunny clearing where the fallen leaves were dry and warm. We could hear a few faint gunshots and even farther away the tiny scream of a chain saw. We made love in the leaves, then quickly got dressed again in case passing hunters stumbled on us, and sat listening to the sound of the shifting, settling foliage.

Maureen and I had been spending much of our free time together, but the agitated noises of the city always surrounded us. Now, as we sat in the isolated silence of the Vermont woods, I became acutely aware of what a quiet person she could be.

"What are you thinking about?" I asked.

"Oh . . . just how nice it is here."

I tended to regard silence between two people who were together as an acknowledgment of failure, and I wasn't sure if Maureen's quiet was natural, the result of some deep inner tranquillity, or if I simply lacked the words to start the conversations she wanted to have.

We drove down out of the mountains and turned north again. The narrower valleys had sunk completely into bluish shadow. The air had grown more chilly, and the fading sun cast a slanting pink light along the ridges. I told Maureen we should look for a motel, but the first few we passed all had their NO VACANCY lights illuminated. It seemed like a strange coincidence. A few miles farther on we approached a motel that appeared to have rooms available. It was a ramshackle place, a row of unadorned cinder-block rooms fronted by a metal porch rail, less desirable than its more charming competitors down the road, but there were only a few cars parked in the lot. Our luck had held. Maureen gave me a relieved look. I reciprocated with a reassuring smile. I wanted her to understand that I was a capable provider, someone she could count on to overcome unforeseen setbacks.

I pulled up in front of the office and got out. The office door was locked. I rang the bell. After a long wait a man opened the door. He had a wolfish beard and under it, tucked into his shirt collar, a stained napkin. My smile now was one of thankfulness, and I expected, since we were about to engage in a mutually satisfactory transaction, to be greeted with a pleased, welcoming expression. Instead, when I requested a room for the night, the man scowled.

"Can't you read?" he asked. He pointed to a handwritten sign stuck in the corner of a window. It said NO VACANCY!!!

My hopeful smile evaporated. I hadn't noticed the sign. Feeling stupid, I apologized. The man shook his head and began to close the door. I asked, "Why's everyone booked?"

"Leaf season," he said.

"Do you know a place that would have a room?"

He exhaled in exasperation. "It's peak color," he said. "Every place in the state's full this weekend." He closed the door in my face.

We drove on into the twilight, but while we stopped at several more inns, none of them had a vacancy and all of the owners were as unsympathetic as the man with the wolfish beard. I was told, in tones of pitiless disdain, that the advent of peak color triggered a tourist onslaught, that this was the busiest time of the year, that most people had booked their rooms a year in advance, on their trip up during the previous leaf season, that to have traveled to Vermont on this particular weekend without a reservation was an act of lunacy. Night fell, and passing through the small villages where farsighted guests smugly unpacked their cars in the lighted parking lots of trim motels, I experienced a feeling of hopelessness. To ward it off, I tried to maintain a level of confident banter, but my voice sounded hollow and I eventually stopped. Maureen was quiet but patient. She seemed to continue to think I was resourceful enough to conjure up a solution. Three hours later, after driving all the way across the state in search of lodging, we ended up in a small town just over the Vermont–New Hampshire border. Maureen pointed out a busy tavern.

"Let me go in there and ask," she said. "Maybe the bartender knows somewhere we could stay."

I sat in the car and waited. Minutes passed. People entered the tavern. Others left. The interior of the car began to turn cold. I opened the door to go look for Maureen, and just then she came out of the tavern with a large man who, like the scowling motelier, had a beard that grew up almost to his eyes. He nodded at me and climbed into his car, a black Cougar.

"Follow him," Maureen said. "He said he knows a place just outside town."

The Cougar rolled through the streets, reached the edge of the town, and accelerated up into the mountains. It was moving very fast, its red taillights disappearing around the curves, and I had to push our four-cylinder rental car to keep up. The road was pitch-black. Our passing headlights swept the silvery trees that crowded either side.

"Why do we have to follow him?" I asked.

"He said the directions were too complicated."

The Cougar continued to climb. We seemed to be heading into remote country. There were no houses, no stores, no streetlights. The only signs of human habitation were occasional roadside clusters of oversized country mailboxes looming up in the dark.

"I thought you said he said it was just a few miles outside town."

"That's what he said."

The Cougar raced ahead into the blackness. I began to wonder if the man had told the truth. I looked at Maureen. She seemed calm. I decided to say nothing.

We drove on and on, and I grew increasingly anxious. The trip was taking too long. There was no motel way out here. I became certain that the man in the Cougar was an opportunistic criminal who had realized when he heard Maureen asking in the tavern about lodging that he could lure us into the mountains and rob and kill us. A girl I had gone to high school with and a distant cousin of mine had both been killed while hitchhiking by the men who had picked them up, one in the South, one out West. Surely such men existed in New Hampshire as well, men who were otherwise law-abiding, men with jobs and maybe even families, who would act on impulse to murder a stranger if they felt confident they could get away with it.

I decided we should write off the Cougar, turn around, and drive through the night back to the city, and I was about to broach this plan to Maureen when the Cougar's turn signal flashed. The car pulled into a long driveway, and I had to make a decision. Do we trust this stranger? I hadn't even gotten a good look at the man, much less talked to him. I'd had no opportunity to take his measure. I looked at Maureen. Her expression showed only relief that we had arrived. I couldn't decide if my intuition was paranoid or shrewd. Unwilling to appear cowardly, I followed the other car into the driveway and up to an immense dark house.

The man in the Cougar honked his horn, a light came on, he waved and drove off, and a couple appeared at the door—this man too had a beard, but kept his upper lip clean-shaven in the manner of the Amish—and welcomed us into a book-lined room where a fire burned in the fireplace. The house, the couple explained, was on an estate that had been converted to a country club. Off-season, while the members were away, the couple, who acted as the caretakers, made a little extra money by quietly taking in guests. They led us up to a bedroom with hand-stenciled wallpaper and a four-poster bed. A radiator beside the window hissed cheerily. We slept well, and when we rose in the morning and pulled back the curtains we saw deer grazing on a fairway strewn with brilliant leaves.

It had all been Maureen's doing. She was a person who trusted that things would work out and found that, because of her trust, more often than not they did. She'd had the pluck, the faith in herself and in strangers that I hadn't had, and as a result we had been rewarded that night in New Hampshire in a way that felt almost magical. Maureen no longer seemed elusive to me. She seemed fearless, carefree, and lucky, and she made me think that if I combined my luck with hers, if the trusting and the skeptic joined forces, we would both do quite well indeed.

Chapter 6

We all from time to time feel lucky, feel we are to be favored by chance, and most of us secretly, even shamefully, believe we can enhance our luck with totems, prayers, private rituals, and magical thinking. We want to protect ourselves from the vagaries of chance, the chilling randomness that dictates who is and who isn't the victim of falling trees, flying bullets, drunk drivers, birth defects, tumors, viruses, lightning, that determines who does and who doesn't receive the sandwich containing the spoiled bacon, the ticket on the plane that will hit wind sheer when landing in Denver, the fatally incorrect diagnosis from the overworked emergency-room resident. It is easy to dismiss luck as a delusion, a superstitious fantasy manufactured in some primitive layer of the human mind. But what separates magical thinking from positive thinking? Aren't they both simply manifestations of our attitude? Isn't a belief in luck simply a way of expressing our faith in ourselves?

Luck, I felt, was on my side that year. The UN executive Maureen was sharing an apartment with was recalled to New Zealand in the fall, and Maureen had to find a new place to live. She was about to put down a security deposit on a tiny and expensive studio with a bathtub in the kitchen when I told her she shouldn't commit herself to such a huge expense. She should instead, I said, move in with me. I don't think this idea had occurred to her. She seemed surprised and slightly hesitant, as if she felt she were giving up options she had assumed she would keep open, but she agreed and moved into my apartment.

I was living at the time in an old town house near Riverside Park. My apartment had only one room, but it was large, with a high ceiling and a fireplace and a rectangular bay window through which you could see, at the end of the block, a slice of the river. It was also, although it was on a quiet street, extremely noisy from time to time. The man who lived above me worked in the theater and would return home late every night, just after I'd gone to bed, and unwind by dancing for an hour or more in his cowboy boots. The teenagers from the tenement on the corner congregated at night on the stoop of the town house because in front of it stood a streetlight into which they could illegally wire the oversized radios they used to fill the entire cavernous block with the monotonously driving rhythms of salsa. The town house next door was a home for quadriplegic children, and sometimes late at night they would begin to moan inconsolably, their wailing and keening penetrating the brick walls with a horrible ghostliness.

These were all resolutely intractable problems. I once threatened the dancer with a hammer, but it produced only a temporary quiet. A rain of eggs and glass bottles would drive the teenagers away, but they would return, sometimes the next night, sometimes an hour later. And nothing could be done to quiet the haunted quadriplegic children. Most mornings I would stagger out of the apartment glassy-eyed from having been kept awake by one or more of these disruptions, thinking, *Anything, anything, God, for one good night's sleep.*

Maureen scarcely seemed to notice the noise, and under her influence, distracted by her presence, I was bothered by it less. Maureen also taught me, in those first few months together, to enjoy caviar and raw fish, to cook with garlic, to appreciate a good Brouilly and Schubert's piano music for four hands. But her superior sophistication, foretold in that order of mussels on our first date, never felt daunting. We all learn from those we love; they shape us into what we are, and their impact is the most profound when it is unintentional. And I influenced her as well. I edited her articles, taught her how to ski, drove the car, read the maps. I tended to set the agenda and make the decisions.

My father had always wanted to be a writer. He had published three books of political science and written short stories, plays, and a novel (as well as numerous Kiplingesque poems) that never found a publisher, and when I was very young he instilled the same ambition in me. I never seriously considered any other career. At the age of twenty-five, having written a novel of my own that had failed to find a publisher, I lost my enthusiasm for the life of the unheralded artist and persuaded the editors of a big news magazine to give me an entry-level job. By the time Maureen and I began living together, my initial euphoria at having been hired by such a prestigious publication had faded. The corporate ladder was crowded, the upward climb a slow one. I was seething with ambition, I worked hard, I showed initiative and diligence, but I had been unable to translate this drive into any measure of recognition. "Patience, my dear boy, patience," one of the editors, a gay alcoholic whose hands trembled when he passed around cables at the weekly story meetings, would tell me when I pushed for bigger assignments. But I had no patience. I was restless. I had various schemes to move to South America or the Middle East. I would become a freelance writer. Life, I believed then, needed to be exotic and dangerous. Otherwise, what was the point? How could you enjoy comfort if you hadn't endured hardship, food if you hadn't gone without? How could you appreciate tranquillity unless you had first *stared death in the face*?

Maureen was the first woman I had known who saw these schemes as something more than adolescent fantasies. They seemed reasonable to her. They seemed plausible. After all, she had lived her own life in a similar fashion. In taking these notions seriously, she took me seriously. She enhanced my idea of myself and I felt, in her presence, older and more worldly. The feeling was deepened when I was around her friends. They were from Wellington and Cairo and Barcelona. They worked in senior positions at the UN and wrote for the British newspapers, and over dinner at Greek restaurants, the tables crowded with bottles of retsina and overflowing ashtrays, we discussed the viability of a nuclear freeze and Jeane Kirkpatrick's declaration that authoritarian governments were preferable to Communist ones.

Maureen, serene in her assumption that I knew the direction my life was taking, didn't understand why I continued to see Dr. Lipsman. Lipsman was a psychologist. I had gone to see him because around the time I started working at the newsmagazine, I began to suffer from chronic nausea. I awoke with a queasy stomach, the tug of imminent gastrointestinal revolt, and the sensation pursued me for the entire day. The slightest provocation——the metallic stench of a homeless person squeezing in next to me on the crowded subway, the sight of a dog gulping down a rancid sausage it had pulled from the garbage——made me gag. I joked to myself that I was suffering from "existential anxiety," but at the time, far from feeling disgusted by the pointlessness of human existence, I was entranced by its possibilities, and the truth was I had absolutely no idea what was responsible for these symptoms. I hoped Lipsman, a noted Freudian quoted periodically in *The New York Times,* could provide some insight.

Lipsman had initially sent me to an internist to see if my problem was physiological. The internist fed me a barium milk shake, took X rays of my stomach and esophagus for ulcers and tumors, and, finding nothing, told me, "You're going to need some stern sessions with Dr. Lipsman." These sessions took place in Lipsman's suite of gloomy offices in the rear of the ground floor of a white-brick apartment building in Murray Hill. Lipsman was a short, paunchy man in his late fifties, bald except for a fringe of white hair that he kept extremely short and that emphasized the angled panels of his cranium. He dressed in corduroy jackets, khaki slacks, and chewed leather canoeing shoes and delivered his observations—many of which were, as the radiologist predicted, "stern," for Lipsman was an impatient, opinionated, unforgiving man—with a distinctively nasal Port Jefferson honk. He believed in free association. At the start of each session he fastidiously placed a fresh paper doily on the headrest of his nubby olive couch and then invited me to lie back and let the associations issue forth while he sat behind me, occasionally eating a lunch of cold cereal.

Lipsman quickly determined that my problems were profound. I was, he believed, suffering from "suppressed rage" at my parents for childhood dislocations—the moves, by the time I was five, from Yokosuka to Long Beach to Washington to Accra back to Washington and then on to Taichung. When I told him ours was a happy family, that I admired my parents and didn't hold them in the least responsible for whatever anxieties that might afflict me, he laughed scornfully. The extent of my denial amused him. The repression, he said, was so thorough, so ironclad, so seamless, that it was literally making me ill. I told him I didn't think my problems were that severe. "Your problems are so serious that even if you were terminally ill with cancer I would recommend you continue treatment," he told me.

At most of the sessions, however, I merely ended up complaining about how frustrated I felt at work. I told Lipsman of my plans to move abroad. They didn't seem *entirely* unreasonable. I had one friend who had gone off to São Paulo, another was in Phnom Penh, a third in Paris. Several established foreign correspondents I knew had gotten their start this way. Lipsman insisted I was deluding myself.

"You're running from your problems," he said. "You think you can escape them but you can't. You'll carry them with you. I don't want to hear about your problems at work. Tell me about your father."

Maureen did not then believe, though this was just the tack she took when our marriage ran into trouble, that I had any emotional problems that warranted therapy. And she was unimpressed with my suggestion that I was simply undergoing an exercise in self-examination that any intelligent person would find interesting and productive. She rejected the idea that she might profit from a similar inquiry. She thought that I was wasting my time and money seeing Lipsman, that the entire enterprise was foolish and typically, naively American. But the therapeutic process, with the promise it offered of identifying external causes for my nature, of letting me off the hook, in a sense, for being who I was, proved too tantalizing. Lipsman's conviction that I was deeply troubled seemed so authoritative, I had no choice, I felt, but to yield to it.

After several months of scouring my pleasant, mostly sunny childhood memories for the fragments of darkness that would support Lipsman's tragic Freudian scenario, I had what I thought was a breakthrough. It came in the form of a dream in which I, as a child, approached my father and he turned on me with a wrathful expression and then erupted in a blistering, terrible rage. I had never had a dream like this, and when Wednesday afternoon arrived I hurried to Lipsman's office and, like a retriever laying a dead bird at his master's feet, presented it to the psychologist. He grunted and asked me how I interpreted it. I was ready for the question. In fact, I had the whole matter worked out. Clearly, I said, the dream revealed my own guilt, and my fear of my father's anger, at betraying the family in therapy.

"No, no, no," he said. "It's projection. It's your anger, your rage. But since you still feel guilty about the rage you feel toward your father, you cannot allow yourself to acknowledge it, and so you project it onto your father. This enables you to experience the guilt but still suppress the underlying rage that causes it. You see?" He sighed. "We still have much serious work to do."

I sighed too. I felt defeated, a retriever whose master kicks the dead bird away. The problem was that, try as I might—and, deferring to Lipsman's expertise, I did try—I couldn't bring myself to swallow Lipsman's thesis of suppressed rage. Lipsman was insisting that I feel sorry for myself. Indeed, self-pity, it had become clear, was a precondition I had to meet before the *real* therapy could begin. But the fact was that I didn't feel sorry for myself. I believed what I'd always believed, that we'd been golden.

Two months after the failed interpretation of the dream I decided there was no point in continuing treatment. When I told Lipsman this, he shrugged. "I think you're making a big mistake," he said, "but it's your life."

I settled down on the nubby olive couch for the last time, my head on the fresh doily. I stared up, for the last time, at the whorled pattern of pinpricks in the soundproofed ceiling. Lipsman said nothing. I sat up.

"Aren't you going to give me your conclusions as a way of wrapping things up?" I asked.

"My conclusions are useless," he said. "Anyway, you already know what I think."

He was right, I did. I left after ten minutes, although Lipsman, in accordance with the economics of his profession, charged for the full hour. About a month later I realized that the nausea had disappeared. I never could decide whether the treatment was responsible.

Chapter 7

Six months after Maureen and I started living together, the magazine I was working for sent me to Boston to fill in for an employee who had, in turn, been dispatched to London. The assignment, temporary but indeterminate, was my chance to prove myself. The magazine put me up in a room at the Ritz. Semipermanent hotel existence, those first few months in Boston, seemed terribly grand, life the way it was lived by movie stars or exiled Iranian aristocrats. The hotel staff greeted me by name. I had a favorite table by the window in the café, and there in the mornings, dressed for work in a navy blazer and gray flannel slacks, I drank piping hot coffee, ate crustless toast off a silver rack, and read newspapers folded so crisply they might have been pressed.

Because it was late spring, the Ritz overflowed with parents who had come to watch their children graduate from Harvard and MIT and Boston University. The groups they formed, the fathers tapping their wineglasses with their dessert spoons prior to making toasts in crowded restaurants, the mothers posing the extended family for photographs among the bursting azaleas of the Garden, were festive and ebullient. The parents, whose lives had long since been restricted by the choices they had made, seemed to reexperience through their children a sense of the world as a place of vast possibilities, and they all contributed to the over-powering feeling of promise that gripped me that spring. My career, I felt sure that spring, was about to take off, and I was alone and free in a vibrant, gleaming, romantic city.

But the novelty of the arrangement soon faded. The work was routine—it consisted primarily of telephoning professors and executives and politicians for information and quotes to be filed in reports that were shipped off to New York, where they usually vanished—and the office was small. Aside from me, there was a secretary; the woman who managed it, a fretful chain-smoker who had a raucously nervous laugh; and a third woman, unmarried and embittered, who closed her door every Monday afternoon for a therapy session she conducted over the telephone with an analyst in New York. I began to understand why my predecessor had been so desperate to get to London. As for the Ritz, I got tired of living in a small room furnished with colonial reproductions, tired of the endless waits for room-service meals delivered by waiters who were, as one of them told me, forbidden from initiating personal conversations with guests, tired of putting on the jacket and tie required for meals in the café, tired of evening walks around Beacon Hill peering into chintz-swagged parlor windows at uproarious parties.

Also, I missed Maureen. I saw her most weekends, flying down to New York on the Eastern shuttle. Maureen's life, which had seemed so eventful and rewarding a year earlier, had become slightly aimless. There had been a change of editors at the Paris newspaper to which she had been contributing and the assignments she received had dwindled off. She looked for research jobs and wrote service articles for women's magazines. But she had time on her hands, and I suggested she come up to Boston.

Since my bills at the Ritz had by now become obscene, I took it upon myself to save the company some money by moving into a small furnished apartment on Marlborough Street. Maureen joined me there, first for a weekend, then for longer and longer stays, and it was there, in an anonymously furnished room in a city in which we were strangers and on which we had no claim, during a period of uncertainty, transience, and heightened isolation, that we decided to get married.

Like everyone else, I can remember some moments of my life, often trivial moments, with microscopic specificity, while there are other moments, at times crucial ones, that I cannot remember at all. This could be due to the vagaries of memory. Or it could reflect calculation: memory's effort to hide from us, for our own good, the discouraging past. As I recall, Maureen raised the idea of marriage first. Maureen, however, remembers my suggesting it. What I do remember vividly——as we walked along the damp, leaf-plastered streets those autumn evenings or sat in the snug room while the wind off the Charles moaned down the chimney——was how appropriate, how compelling, how natural the prospect of marriage seemed. I had not thought marriage was on my calendar for that year. I hadn't expected it or planned for it. I had certainly never identified it as a goal I intended to attain by the age of twenty-eight. But suddenly it beckoned. Marriage, to this sweet, elusive Englishwoman six years older than myself, seemed right.

Looking back, my reasons seem much more solid, considered, and defensible than my father's for marrying my mother at the age of twenty-one. We had been living together for more than a year, and since at the time I subscribed to my father's view of history and life as progressive, marriage appeared to be the next step forward. It would perpetuate a sense of directed motion. My wife was the prettiest and gentlest woman I had ever been involved with. We found the same things amusing. Maureen, for her part, wanted to have a child; motherhood was the last adventure awaiting her. And we loved each other.

I was the first of my friends to get married. We were, for the most part, children of the generation who had married in the fifties. Our parents had been raised in the Depression; our fathers, many of them, had fought in Korea or in World War II. They had returned home to find that the GI Bill enabled them to go to college; GI loans gave them access to their own new houses in the suburbs; and the departure, forced or voluntary, of women from the jobs they'd held during the war gave them access to wives. They didn't need to wait, as *their* parents had, until they had reached their late twenties and established themselves; they could start their families immediately. And they did. Marriage was almost a social necessity. Remaining unmarried made it difficult to join and certainly to flourish in the top corporations. The unmarried were suspected of loose morals, immaturity, bohemian tendencies, homosexuality.

The children of this generation, when they came of age, considered marriage a dated bourgeois convention. Why get married when you could live together? Why buy when you can rent? Marriage, for many of the people I knew, seemed an option to be considered only if you were interested in having children, and most of the people I knew at that time had no desire to propagate themselves. The men especially were content with the configuration their lives had assumed in their mid-twenties: a job; some buddies; sports; a succession of girlfriends who in the end always proved, in their opinion, either too neurotic, too hard, too plain, or too dumb to qualify as marriage material.

Such a life always struck me as so shallow and narrow it was virtually pointless. I aspired to marriage. And to family life. To me a marriage without children made no more sense than bachelorhood. Without children, I felt, there was no real family. There was no consanguinity, no shared blood, and no heirs and descendants, the future generations who console you on your deathbed and offer the one intimation of immortality that to me has any logic. Without children, you simply had two people who had signed a binding contract to share their wealth and remain sexually faithful. Children created the family, and the family, in turn, created the one place—a portable place, a psychic place, invisible and intangible but a place nonetheless—where you truly belonged.

I was chronically, congenitally restless in those days. I was, in fact, getting married out of restlessness. For me marriage was a way not of settling down but of moving on. What had always made me restless was the feeling that I didn't truly belong where I happened to be. The desire to wander didn't motivate me. The search for the place I could call home did.

Maureen was Jewish. She considered this a matter more of identity and heritage than faith; her religious impulses were limited to the desire to attend synagogue on Yom Kippur and to serve a seder on Passover. Nonetheless, she wanted us to have a Jewish wedding. It was, she said, important. I had little enthusiasm for this proposal, and as she explained the ceremony to me—the *chuppah,* the Hebrew prayers, the smashing of the wineglass—even the negligible enthusiasm I had managed to muster diminished. None of these rituals had anything to do with *me*. It seemed disrespectful that someone to whom they meant nothing would perform them. I would feel like an intruder, a fraud. But I decided not to mention any of this. If my wife-to-be wanted a Jewish wedding, I would go along. Back in New York, Maureen found a rabbi who would perform interfaith marriages, and she scheduled an appointment for us all to talk, to see if we were on the same wavelength.

We met at the rabbi's apartment. The turquoise mezuzah nailed to the door frame reminded me again how alien I found Judaism. I rang the bell, one of those mechanical coiled-spring bells that give a harsh double clang. A woman opened the door so quickly it seemed as if she had been waiting just inside. She introduced herself as the rabbi's wife. I started to make conversation, but she refused to be drawn in. Her duties did not encompass hospitality. Saying nothing, she led us into the living room. It was small and dark, low-ceilinged, lined with books, and overlooking a highway that seethed with traffic. The rabbi sat in a corner reading, oblivious to the noise from the road. I had expected an authoritative, even grim figure, but he was affable, a young bearded man, slightly overweight, who wore blue-tinted glasses and a yarmulke.

I had also expected the rabbi to grill us about our intentions and beliefs, our plans for the religion of our children, but he mentioned none of that. He seemed almost eager to please. He never stopped smiling. Leaning forward in his Naugahyde armchair, revealing a strip of duct tape used to repair a split seam, the rabbi said he had no problem with interfaith marriages. He believed, he said, that we all worshiped the same God. Maureen and I said we agreed.

The rabbi asked me my views on the nature of love. I told the rabbi I thought love was the highest emotion to which human beings could aspire. It required sacrifice, and sacrifice gave it in turn a spiritual dimension. I said I thought God perhaps existed, as an organizing intelligence for the universe, but that He was remote and unknowable and the idea that He would reveal Himself on occasion to a select group of people and would be vain and petty enough, childish enough, to insist that they worship Him, to be obsessed with their flattery and obeisance, seemed to me to insult the very idea of a Supreme Being. I said, summoning up the reasonable Unitarian agnosticism with which I had been raised, that I thought human beings had imagined God out of what was best in themselves and that was love. God was the idealization of human love or, to put it another way, love was the presence of the divine within us.

The rabbi beamed and nodded. Maureen looked at me with affection. I sat back, pleased with my eloquence. What I didn't know then, what I didn't ask myself, was whether these were merely ideas I entertained or convictions I held. But the rabbi didn't ask me that either.

"I'll be happy to marry you," he said.

Historically, divorce rates have risen in times of prosperity. Social reactionaries—the fastidious journalist on the Sunday-morning talk show, the berobed Virginia minister with the sonorous voice, the Waspish Amherst neoconservative—attribute this to the godlessness and spinelessness and self-indulgence that affluence supposedly breeds; the decline of organized religion, they argue, corresponds to the rise in divorce. But another explanation is that prosperity frees people from their financial dependence on each other. Miserable couples who would have previously remained together only because they were forced to—either by circumstance or religious stricture—no longer do.

Aren't all these people who decry the "divorce culture," who instruct the miserable to quit complaining and endure their misery, willfully ignoring what is supposed to be the other great social malaise of our time, the epidemic of "dysfunctional families"? Isn't one of the great preoccupations of the twentieth century—a theme that runs through literature and psychology from Freud and Eugene O'Neill to William Styron and the contemporary proponents of the quest for the "inner child"—the tragedy of the unhappy family forced to remain together? Isn't it possible to view divorce, for all its attendant trauma, as a progressive, even healthy development?

Nonetheless, only the rich, more interested in wealth than in happiness, plan for divorce even as they get married and, when it occurs, seem to accept it as a matter of course. The rest of us, like

criminals who refuse to think about prison in the midst of committing their felonies, never do. It would incapacitate us.

That December, eighteen months after we had met, we were
married. I was still on assignment in Boston, but we continued to
consider New York home, and we held the ceremony there. On
the day of the wedding I rose early in the new apartment we had
just rented. Near Penn Station and the central post office, it was,
we discovered after we signed the lease, even noisier than our previous apartment. A guard dog in a fenced-in lot at the end of the
block barked all night. Long-haul trucks rumbled down the street
in the predawn hours, and all of them hit with a percussive bang a
pothole just outside our building. We'd been there only a couple of
months, and had been spending most of that time in Boston, but I
was ready to move again. The apartment, full of unpacked boxes
and reeking of paint, begged to be abandoned even before it was
fully occupied.

I awoke that morning cocky and impatient, brimming with
confidence and excitement, but I was also feeling slightly vague, as
if I were about to begin a journey to a place about which I had
heard only rumors. Maureen had spent this last night of her unmarried life in her sister's hotel room, but my sister, her husband,
and an uncle had stayed with me, sleeping on the floor among the
scattered boxes, inhaling paint fumes. I brewed coffee, showered
and shaved, and then dressed in the rented morning suit that for
some inexplicable reason I had decided I should wear, and we all
set off in a taxi through the cold, wet streets.

The foul weather made the warmth inside the Murray Hill
town house where we had arranged to hold the wedding feel even
more inviting. It was owned by a gay couple—one was thin, with
graying hair; the other, burly, mustachioed, and voluble, resem-
bled the youthful Teddy Roosevelt—who rented it out for such

occasions and managed the festivities. They had suggested the caterer and the pianist, provided the silverware and the folding chairs, and lit the fat white candles that flickered in the windows. The town house was too narrow to accommodate a front parlor. The main door, painted red, opened into an anteroom with a black-and-white tile floor where the pianist played Schubert on a baby grand that glowed like obsidian. Beyond that, in a carpeted hallway, a carved white newel-post anchored the staircase.

Maureen's parents arrived at the same time I did. They had flown in, with her younger sister, the day before, and we greeted each other with a familiarity that succeeded only in emphasizing how unknown we all were to one another. Complete strangers were about to become my close relatives. Although I had met my prospective in-laws only the previous night, I liked them both. Maureen's father was a generous, fretful man who, along with his brothers, ran a salmon-smoking company in London. Her mother was sarcastic and opinionated and got a kick out of imitating American accents. Although she now wore a wig, she had been quite beautiful when she was young, and even in her sixties she retained—the way the trace of a regional accent will linger in someone who has lived for years in the city—mildly coquettish airs. They were both the children of Russian Jews who had fled the pogroms around Kiev at the turn of the century and wound up in London's East End. Maureen had shown me pictures of these ancestors, fierce Asiatic men with skullcaps and wild beards, stout women in embroidered smocks. It was an exotic bloodline.

A wedding is a ceremony of acceptance as well as a good-bye party, and never in my life have I felt as fully and as widely accepted as I did that day. My parents and sisters and uncles and cousins, friends from high school and college and work all descended on the town house to see me off on this voyage. We all gathered around the newel-post at the foot of the staircase, waiting for Maureen to descend, and when she did I led her into the rear parlor, its glazed lemon walls lit with candlelight, and stood under the purple canopy with the gold piping held up by four friends as the rabbi pronounced the benediction in Hebrew. When it was over, I stamped on the wineglass swaddled in its linen napkin, and it made a rich explosive crunch. I was christening our marriage, and just as at the launch of a new boat the flushed and grinning crowd burst into enthusiastic applause.

In my favorite photograph from the wedding, a close-up, my wife and I are talking as we dance. She wears a slender garland of apple blossoms. Her small hands, extending from the lace sleeves of her cream-colored dress, cup the back of my head, her gray-green eyes, in which you can see faintly reflected candlelight, hold mine, and she is laughing at whatever it is I am saying. It's the memory of my making her laugh, of my making this one woman truly happy on this one day, that the photograph evokes.

It began to snow late that afternoon, which slowed our progress when we set out in the early evening for the inn in the Berkshires where we had reserved a room. By the time we arrived, the long drive through the falling snow, following the wedding and the reception, with its dancing, champagne, and cigars, had left me fatigued. The innkeeper expected us, knew we were on our honeymoon, and had set a fire in the fireplace. I lit it. He had left us a bottle of champagne. We drank it, made love in front of the fire, and fell asleep under a thick comforter with the wind rattling the shutters, but for some reason not only did my wife consider our wedding night a disappointment, but she always held it against me. She had expected something from the evening that I had failed to give her. She never told me what it was and I never asked, but in later years she would refer to it obliquely, this mysterious disappointment that to her prefigured the others to come.

Chapter 8

When the Christmas holidays were over, Maureen and I returned to Boston. That spring, after my temporary assignment in the city had lasted exactly one year, I received a call from the company's head of personnel. He informed me that the man he had sent to London would not be returning and that he had found someone else to permanently take the position I had been filling. I was to return to New York to resume my old duties. When I asked why I wasn't getting the job, he explained, confidentially, that the woman who ran the Boston office had complained in an evaluation that I had an "attitude problem." I worked industriously on projects I thought were important or interesting, she said, but if I considered an assignment pointless I was likely to give it short shrift.

We are all fundamentally oblivious of the way we appear to others, and if we could see ourselves the way others see us, it would unsettle us even more than hearing the sound of our own voices on a tape recorder. Talking to the head of personnel, I was stunned by the fact that such a wide gulf existed between the way this woman, the manager, saw me and the way I saw myself. I had thought I was cheerful and cooperative, friendly and hopeful. During my year in Boston I may have made one or two errors of judgment, but who didn't when they were young? I had also worked long hours and displayed ingenuity and resourcefulness and initiative. I had, I felt, exceeded expectations. But, it now turned out, I had been deluding myself.

I began to protest. I could distinguish between the worthless and the worthwhile, I said. That was a valuable trait. It revealed a sense of discrimination on my part. How did it constitute "attitude"?

"Don't challenge the evaluation," the head of personnel said. "That's just showing more attitude."

Enraged, I left the office, crossed Copley Square, and headed for the river. The sky was overcast, and the low cloud cover blotted out all shadows. A late winter storm the day before had covered the city with six inches of dense snow, but the temperature had risen immediately, and now the entire world seemed wet. Water dripped from the eaves of the Back Bay brownstones and trickled out of drainpipes. It leaked from melting piles of shoveled snow, ran in the streets, and pooled at intersections. A dank, spongy fog enveloped the black trees along the river, which was lead-colored, sluggish, and opaque. As I made my way along one of the paths a young man in a leather flight jacket came toward me and, instead of passing, stopped. He had a narrow face and eyes that fluttered nervously.

"I want to suck you off," he said.

I stared at him.

"We can go in the bathrooms over there," he added.

In an instant my sense of aggrievement was transformed into a focused and irresistible urge to inflict pain. I roared something vile and leaped on the man. We rolled in the wet snow. I tried to punch his face. He thrashed his arms in defense. He was not strong—I can remember the feel of his thin shoulders twisting frantically inside his flight jacket—and I landed several blows before he scrambled away, crying with fright and indignation, and splattered off through the snow. I was gasping for breath. I turned over onto my back and stared up. Water trickled down my collar and into my sleeves. It soaked my shoes and pants and the back of my coat. Eventually my breathing returned to normal, but I continued to lie there, motionless, studying the network of dripping black branches overhead.

When I returned from Boston I went in to see the head of my department, a small, precise man, urbane but colorless, who, in what I always took to be an attempt to compensate for that deficiency, wore gaudy bow ties. His office looked out on Madison Avenue. A building boom was under way and the rattling, grinding sounds of construction poured in through his open window. The department head let me know that Boston had afforded me my one shot at moving ahead within the corporation. I'd had my opportunity there and had been unable to make it work for me; no other opportunities would be forthcoming. I would not be fired, but I needed to accept a future without the hope of promotion. I felt the floor slide under me. When the department head said something more I couldn't hear him. The construction noise seemed to have overwhelmed the room, but that may instead have been the turmoil in my mind.

"What?" I said.

"Some people are just not lucky at a certain place," he said. "Those people need to try their luck somewhere else."

For three weeks I sat in a windowless office feeling sorry for myself, and then I quit.

Later that summer, at my insistence, Maureen finally made an appointment with a neurologist. The previous fall, when I was still in Boston, she'd taken a plane up from New York one Friday afternoon, and when she arrived she complained that something was wrong with her left arm. She had difficulty fully extending it, and there was an almost imperceptible tremor in her smallest finger. She had brought a portable typewriter with her on the flight, and she assumed she had strained her arm carrying it.

But after several weeks the tremor hadn't gone away. If anything, it appeared slightly more pronounced. She had seen a doctor who proposed a number of possible causes—a pulled ligament, stress, neurological disorder—and urged a month of rest. When, after the month of rest, the symptoms persisted, we decided it had to be a pinched nerve. That spring, upon our return to New York, she visited a chiropractor, who stretched her limbs and cracked her spine, and an acupuncturist, who inserted needles into her neck and shoulders. None of these remedies worked either. An undercurrent of dread stole through me whenever I thought about Maureen's symptoms—dread combined with a bitter sense of futility and injustice. She was *young,* we had just gotten married, we had other problems to deal with. But when I talked to Maureen I remained upbeat, even dismissive. It was nothing, I assured her. Whatever it was, it was nothing.

Still, I insisted she see a neurologist, just to rule out certain possibilities. Since she was apprehensive, I accompanied her on the visit. The neurologist was a young, bearded man with black-framed glasses, cold hands, and a stiff clinical manner. He examined Maureen briefly, studied her balance, had her squeeze a rubber ball, and felt the tremor pulsing deep within her arm. Then he invited us to sit down across from his desk.

"Your symptoms are consistent with Parkinson's disease," he said.

For the second time that summer, the floor shifted. I stared at the doctor in disbelief. Maureen couldn't have Parkinson's disease. It was an affliction of the old. Morris Udall, the former congressman, suffered from Parkinson's disease. His tremors were so severe, I had recently read, that it took him half an hour to put his shirt on in the morning. But Morris Udall was in his seventies. He'd led a long, richly rewarding life. My wife was only thirty-four. Thirty-four!

"Maureen's only thirty-four," I said.

"I'm too young to have Parkinson's," she added.

The doctor shrugged. I remember his taking off his glasses and playing with them.

"It's rare at your age, but it does occur," he said. "Anyway, that's why I said your symptoms are consistent with Parkinson's. We don't know what's causing them. We do know what they resemble."

"Well, what else could it be?" I asked.

"Nothing," he said.

The doctor explained that Parkinson's disease was caused by the degeneration of nerve cells within the basal ganglia in the brain, creating a shortage of dopamine, which regulates the flow of neural commands throughout the nervous system. Without an adequate supply of dopamine, the commands arrive irregularly and the patient loses fluidity of movement, the gestures become jerky and spastic. The disease, the doctor continued, was degenerative.

Among older patients the course it ran from initial symptoms to final convulsions took roughly twenty years. When the patient was young, as my wife was, the course varied widely. It was possible for the symptoms to remain in their preliminary form for years. It was even possible, though uncommon, to see some regression.

While at the current time a cure for Parkinson's hadn't been discovered, the doctor went on, drugs could treat the symptoms. The treatment, however, was imperfect. The drugs, which provided an artificial form of dopamine, alleviated rather than eliminated the symptoms. And, unfortunately, many patients developed a tolerance for the drugs. Over time, dosages had to be increased radically.

Researchers, he said, were divided over the question of when young patients like my wife should start taking the drugs. Some felt that the long years of drug use contributed to the violence of the symptoms when the patient reached the late stage, and for that reason they urged delay. Other researchers thought it best to begin treatment early, allowing the patient as many fully functioning years as possible.

"Well, which do you think?" Maureen asked.

"It's up to you," the doctor said. "We don't make the choices. We tell the patient what the choices are."

Maureen was infuriated by his manner, and afterward, on the street outside, she fell into a rage. The arrogant fool, she said. The pompous jerk. He was rude. He was indifferent. What did he know anyway? He was hardly out of medical school. She refused, she said, to return to see him. He was irresponsible and alarmist. I told Maureen I felt she was reacting more to the diagnosis than to the doctor. I tried to be reassuring, but I also wanted to make the point that, if she was ill, I thought she needed to confront the disease rather than run from it. Maureen turned on me. Who the hell was I, she wanted to know, to lecture her on how she should react to something that was happening to her?

I understood why she was angry, and I didn't blame her. She was frightened and, as most of us do, tried to control her fear by turning away from its source. I was frightened too, and sickened. We'd been married less than a year. We'd had plans. I felt guilty for being healthy. I simultaneously wished the disease had afflicted me instead and also felt a great relief that it hadn't—relief that compounded the guilt. I became irritated with myself for paying any attention at all to my feelings when it was my wife who had to face the terrors of the sentence the doctor had imposed. What I felt was irrelevant. From now on, I thought, it was going to be my responsibility, my job, to help her face the trials she would have to endure.

"At least we have our health," my mother would say when our family experienced some setback while I was growing up. "Nothing is more important than your health." When I was younger, and took health for granted, I considered the statement a hopeless cliché, the embodiment of the empty pronouncement, the vacuous thought. And it *was* a commonplace. But the doctor's diagnosis that day made me long for the impossible return of Maureen's health, and I realized that the most profound human truths have an element of the commonplace. A cliché, I thought, remembering the grave simplicity with which my mother used to talk about the preeminent value of health, is a truth you haven't experienced emotionally.

In August, when we were living entirely on my wife's meager income, Maureen learned she was pregnant. While I had always wanted children as well, had always imagined myself as the benevolent patriarchal head of a large and tumultuous household, the desire to become a father, at that particular time in my life, had remained abstract. To begin with, I didn't have a job, much less a career that I could count on to provide a way of supporting my family. And since Maureen and I had moved yet again, to a one-room apartment subdivided into two rooms so narrow it was almost possible to simultaneously touch the opposing walls, we lacked the literal physical space for a child. Our bed and chest of drawers occupied virtually the entire bedroom. We had a shower but no bath, a kitchen but no counter space. Where would we put the crib, the playpen, the high chair, the stroller? Where could we wash and change the baby? Where could we spread out all those huge, brightly colored plastic toys children had begun to require? It seemed at first impossible. Our lives were too small to contain such a large change, too unstable to bear the imposition of this new load.

There was also the question of Maureen's illness. How would it affect, and be affected by, her pregnancy? To get some answers, I went with her to see her gynecologist and obstetrician, Dr. Sherr. Sherr was a trim and clear-eyed man with prematurely white hair who managed to be at once comforting and direct. The Parkinson's disease, he assured us, posed no threat to the baby and would not interfere with Maureen's pregnancy. However, he added, the natural chemical and hormonal changes Maureen could expect to experience during her pregnancy could have an effect on the progress of the illness. These changes might exacerbate the symptoms temporarily. They might speed up the course of the disease. It was, he said, impossible to predict the consequences.

If pregnancy might make Maureen's condition worse, we needed to think about whether or not she should proceed with it. She didn't necessarily have to. But we were married now, which eliminated one conceivable reason to terminate the pregnancy. Furthermore, Maureen wanted a child, and, given the degenerative nature of her condition, she would be better off going through a pregnancy now. It would never be any easier.

Chapter 9

Strangely enough, once their initial shock was over, the startling developments that summer had a bracing effect on me. I felt mobilized and engaged and also, since my wife's illness and pregnancy had in a sense taken my life out of my own hands, released. We had seen the movie *Gallipoli* that year, and I was, I felt, like one of those soldiers during the First World War who hears the trumpet, sees his companions surge out of the trenches, and realizes he now has no choice but to charge forward as well.

Which is what I did. My wife was working at a journal sent free of charge to women doctors. Because she was pregnant, she wanted less demanding work. I took over her job and she found part-time work at another magazine. Then, a month before our daughter was born, I was hired by another newsweekly. Maureen sailed through her pregnancy. My concern about and her fear of her illness receded into the future. It was something we needn't trouble ourselves about for years. Throughout the fall we stayed in the tiny apartment, actually planning to keep the baby in the bottom drawer of the hulking pine dresser we had inherited from the previous tenants, but at the same time I started working for the weekly we acknowledged the insanity of this idea and moved to Brooklyn.

It was, in its heedlessness and impetuosity, characteristic of the way we approached our marriage. We thought of ourselves as eminently flexible; even after Maureen became pregnant we entertained vague and improbable notions of moving to New Delhi or Beirut or Paris. What that turned out to mean was that we were unprepared for the inflexibility that marriage and children impose. Even so, it was largely a happy period. We were both flush with anticipation over what our new life would be like.

Maureen's contractions began one spring night while we were making love. We timed them and called the doctor, who said the intervals were sufficient for us to wait to come to the hospital the following morning. We arrived early, as if our promptness would be rewarded by a prompt delivery, and hiked down the labyrinthine hallways, past the wisecracking orderlies and the wards of bedridden patients in various states of hope and resignation, to the maternity wing, the vast institution's one "happy ward." The other bed in the room Maureen was assigned was already occupied by a plump young woman who was also a patient of Dr. Sherr. Sherr, however, was not on call that weekend, and another doctor in his practice, a jaunty man whose frizzy gray hair was stylishly long, arrived around noon.

There was nothing to do but wait. Maureen was completely absorbed, her fascination tinged with fear, in the insistent movement, the frank restlessness, of the being inside her. I felt largely extraneous. I wandered outside and stared through the soundproof glass at the rows of newborn babies sleeping in the nursery. The obstetrician seemed bored. He flirted halfheartedly with the nurses, leaning against the night station desk. He told me about his plans to attend a tennis camp in Boca Raton. Then he found out that the plump woman's husband, who was even stouter than his wife, worked for a mutual fund, and as the two of them paced the terrazzo hallway, he grilled the young man about the advisability of investing in various upcoming technology issues.

Maureen, I could tell, was nervous, but she acted with admirable calm and fortitude, even when the pain intensified and the doctor decided to give her an epidural. Finally, after about twelve hours, the contractions accelerated. Two nurses wheeled Maureen into the delivery room. A third nurse passed me a set of fog-blue surgical scrubs. In the men's locker room, I fastened the strings of the wash-softened shirt and trousers, tucked my hair into the elasticized cap, slipped the clumsy paper booties over my shoes, and then hurried out to join my wife, whose body was gearing itself to expel a new living creature.

Powerful lights filled the delivery room with an illumination so harsh it seemed smoky. Nurses bustled around the trays of frightening tools, while the doctor, with a look of fierce concentration, crouched between my wife's sheet-draped legs. One of the nurses told me to stand near Maureen's head. By rote I urged her to breathe in, breathe out, push, as I'd been taught to do in the Lamaze class, but the real point of this exercise, I suspected, was to give me, the father, the illusion of usefulness, because by that time I don't think she could even hear me. She was in the grip of contortions so violent they made me feel puny and awestruck, a spectator at the primordial upheaval, the eruption of life, occurring within her body.

The doctor, his frizzy hair stuffed into a bulbous surgical cap, had become violent as well. He barked at my wife to push, then lifted a pair of surgical forceps large enough to be medieval torture implements, thrust them into her, and began wrenching them back and forth. My wife cried out and dug her nails deep into my palm.

The forceps clanked on the floor. The doctor stood up. The tiny creature in his arms was a deep purple, almost a blue. Its hair and skin were smeared with fluid, its limbs and head hung lifelessly. Desperation gripped me as the doctor, instead of holding the baby triumphantly aloft and spanking it, shoved it at a nurse who rushed—in a panic, it seemed to me—to a side table overhung with a track of infrared lights.

What was wrong? I wondered. Why was the baby so blue? Had it strangled on the umbilical cord? The fears I had managed to suppress during most of Maureen's pregnancy—of a harelip, a cleft palate, shriveled limbs, Down's syndrome, the whole nightmarish range of deformities—swarmed over me and I found myself squeezing my wife's hand as tightly as she had been squeezing mine. I looked at the doctor, who was watching the nurse at the side table. The other nurses had become motionless and were watching as well. Everything seemed poised, held in abeyance, as the nurse massaged and stroked the baby, and then, in the one true miracle that I have witnessed, its coloring kindled, progressing from the cold purple to a stormy red and then a deep luminescent pink. Before my eyes my own child, a tiny girl, came alive.

My wife, lying drained and hammered on the operating table, could see none of this, but the sudden stillness in the room alarmed her.

"What's wrong?" she asked. "What's wrong?"

As the nurses swaddled the baby and lifted it out from under the heat lamps, I turned back to the doctor, who now raised both fists in triumph.

"Nothing," I told my wife. "Everything's all right."

As soon as I got back from the hospital I called the store where we had ordered all the furniture for the baby's room and told them to deliver it. We had visited the store months ago and picked out the dresser, the playpen, the crib, the car seat, the high chair, the blankets, the sheets, the towels, the nightgowns, the bibs, the diapers—a complete set of appurtenances accumulated not slowly over time as my belongings had been but in one fell swoop. This small mountain of equipment—the receipt for it ran two and a half pages—had shocked me. It had underscored, even more than the sonogram or the kicking and sloshing going on in my wife's expanding stomach, the seriousness of the responsibilities that the baby's impending arrival entailed. A third party was joining us, and he or she—we couldn't tell the sex from the sonogram—would transform us from a couple into a family. My life, the length of that list made me realize, was about to alter in ways I couldn't imagine.

And possibly, as another incident at the store hinted, in ways I might not want to imagine. When we discussed the question of the delivery of all this stuff with the clerk, a burly Hasidic Jew with genial, shrewd eyes, he had said, "We advise our customers to wait until after the baby is born, just in case . . ."

He knew he didn't need to complete the sentence. The sudden image it produced—grieving parents calling the store to arrange the return of the furniture that had become tragically unnecessary—stirred the fears that attend all parents during pregnancy. But now the baby was born—with ten fingers and ten toes, in the happy phrase—and I called the store to arrange next-day delivery.

We were living then on the top floor of a generously wide brownstone. Ralph and Tina Strafaci, the owners, lived with their two young children on the lower floors. Since we all had to share the same staircase, we often ran into the Strafacis, especially on weekend mornings, going up or down in their bathrobes, their faces swollen and hair tangled from sleep. My wife and I felt we could have dispensed with this familiarity, but otherwise we liked our apartment. Its proportions, in comparison with the apartments we'd had in Manhattan, seemed enormous. The living room, which had two large windows overlooking the broad and peaceful street, was painted dusty rose, its ceiling molding a darker hue of the same color. There was a green-tiled bathroom with a skylight and a trapezoidal tub, a bedroom, and a small study, where, when the deliverymen arrived the day after our daughter was born, I instructed them to install the baby furniture.

The next day I hired, for the first time in my life, a limousine, and on a brilliantly icy March morning arrived at the hospital to escort my wife and daughter, whom we'd decided to call Jessica, home. Maureen seemed frail but undamaged. The sides of Jessica's face had ugly red gouge marks from the forceps that had been used to drag her into the world. Both of them still wore on their wrists the plastic ID bracelets the hospital issued. I helped Maureen ne-gotiate the deep puddle at the curb while the driver held open the car door. The trip back—down the FDR Drive, across the bridge over the heaving slate-colored slab of the East River, through the low-lying industrial flats on the far side of the Heights, and up the wide street near the park to the brownstone with the rose-colored living room—didn't feel like a return. It felt like a departure, an embarkation on the most challenging adventure of them all.

two

Chapter 10

My wife had wanted to have a child, and now I thought she was doing what she wanted to do, staying home and looking after the baby while I worked to pay the bills, which was what I wanted to do. We had agreed it made no sense for her to go back to work. We couldn't understand those mothers who, after six weeks of recuperating from childbirth, hired some woman they didn't know—*a total stranger*—to look after their newborn while they returned to their job. The total stranger, the surrogate mother with whom your child would be spending most of her waking hours, might be depressed or unstable, and was probably down on her luck, uneducated, and without reserves of patience, affection, and energy (not that we didn't have a great deal of sympathy for such people). Why take that risk? we used to ask each other. Why have children at all if you weren't prepared to raise them yourself during those critical early years? What was the point? we wondered. If nothing else, we both agreed, it wasn't fair to the children. So Maureen stayed home. And since she had been working freelance before she became pregnant and therefore did not have a job to return to, the decision was easy. It was, in fact, almost inevitable.

My wife has always made friends easily, and the society in the neighborhood we had moved to was fluid and accessible. Women in my wife's situation—women, that is, who had relinquished careers or at least jobs to raise children—saw themselves as pioneers, and they reached out to other women with similar claims. My wife met them through my daughter's pediatrician and through a play group she joined. Formed ostensibly for the children, its real purpose was to enable the mothers to get together. She became friends with Sharon, the voluptuous and theatrical wife of a local accountant, with Meg, a big-boned, patrician woman whose third child had been born the same week as our daughter, with Emma, a frail, wiry-haired psychologist who subjected everyone's behavior to laborious analytical scrutiny.

There were others, many of them, all vivid and intelligent and opinionated. Dressed in sweatpants and running shoes, their hair tied back in sloppy ponytails, they pushed their meticulously engineered Japanese strollers through the neighborhood's leafy, trash-strewn streets, blocking pedestrian traffic on the sidewalks when they stopped the strollers side by side so their children could reach out and gurgle at one another and they could gossip. They gathered at one another's houses most mornings, these exuberant, glowing mothers, nonchalantly breast-feeding their babies, devouring pains au chocolat and croissants from the local bakery, sharing tips on treating rashes and colds and easing the gum inflammation caused by teething, deploring Ronald Reagan's confrontational attitude toward the Soviet Union and the capitulation of the Democratic Congress to his cuts in welfare programs, and shamelessly, lovingly recounting their child's latest developmental accomplishment. On the weekends, when we husbands were home, we would all get together, on someone's new raw cedar deck, cantilevered out from a back parlor that had been converted into a kitchen, or on a roof garden reached after climbing up a narrow spiral stairway rising through a hole cut in the ceiling, or at a birthday party in the park for one of the kids, its location revealed by following hand-lettered and balloon-festooned signs the parents taped to trees: ERICA GOLDEN'S B'DAY BASH THIS WAY!!

They were lively times, all of us astonished by our own transformation into parents, giddy with the insight into what it had been like for our parents to have raised us, and exhilarated by the beauty, the specificity, the cunning, the cruelty, and the frailty of our little children. Life before our children were born, it seemed to us all, had been pointless. What did childless people do? we wondered. How did they invest their lives with meaning? Such questions baffled us.

I remember one day after coming home from work, while I fixed myself a scotch and Jessica flung herself across the oak floor in her walker and Maureen finished preparing dinner, my wife described how she and three friends had gone for a walk that afternoon, and, because the weather was so gorgeous and their conversation so engrossing, because they were enjoying themselves so thoroughly, they had pushed their strollers all the way to the river and back, a distance of about eight miles. I remember thinking how wonderful it was that my wife was so fully alive, so invigorated by her friends and her child and our hectic existence in the neighborhood that we had chosen so haphazardly. It seems now that, in so many ways, those were the best of times. I wasn't aware of it then, but I later realized that we are capable of identifying the best of times for what they were only after they have passed.

When our daughter was eighteen months old, we moved two blocks to the apartment where we would live for the rest of our marriage, the apartment where my wife and daughter still live today. I loved the apartment and I still do. It seemed to me, when I first saw it, a wonderful place, a place we could grow into and occupy comfortably, the first place I had lived in that did not imply another move in a year or two.

The apartment was in a brownstone, on a sloping street lined with sycamores and locust trees and one massive willow. There were churches, drafty Victorian piles of soot-stained stone, at either end of the block, and on Sunday mornings the plaintively thin sound of the hymns sung by their diminished congregations drifted through our windows. Most of the other buildings on the block were brownstones as well, but ours stood out. It was slightly larger than the rest—the lawyer who had many of them built in the 1890s had set it aside for himself—and as a mark of seigneurial distinction he had carved a lion's head into the low stone wall that enclosed the stoop. The wide eyes and snarling mouth, its fangs dulled by time, fascinated every small child who walked by.

Stu and Mattie Bialer, the two public school teachers who had bought the house for a song ten years earlier—our rent more than covered the mortgage—lived with their three children in the garden and parlor floors. Our apartment occupied the two upper levels. The living room, which had been the original lawyer-builder's master bedroom, had built-in bookcases, a handsome bay window that looked out over a crabapple tree, and a fireplace with a hearth of cracked black marble; my wife was particularly sold on the fireplace. The downstairs bathroom was a florid Victorian extravagance. Its bathtub, sink, and toilet were pear-green, the tiled walls were rose-pink, the tiled floor black. A large stained-glass window in hues of blue and amber depicted a sailboat under scudding clouds. At the back of the house a door in the dining room gave onto the deck, which stood on the roof of the first-floor extension and was shielded from the houses opposite by the massive hickory, a stand of birches, and a weeping cherry tree that every spring flowered for less than a week and then powdered the deck with a blizzard of white petals. Upstairs were three bedrooms, another bathroom, and, something of almost gemstone rarity in New York, a laundry room.

Two lawyers who had previously been living in the apartment moved out when they split up, Stu told me when we came over to look at the place. Before that a gay couple had occupied it; the cherry-red color they had painted the living room walls could still be faintly discerned, beneath the subsequent coats of white, on a gurgling radiator pipe. They too had split up. Prior to the gay couple, Stu said, a graphic artist lived in the apartment with his wife and three children. He had turned the front bedroom into a studio—his children slept in what was now the laundry room—and added the heavily insulated electrical outlets for the soldering guns and heat lamps he used in his work. He took on too many assignments, Stu told us, used amphetamines to stay up late working against deadlines, and eventually suffered a nervous collapse, which also broke up his marriage.

"I hope it doesn't portend anything for you guys," Stu said.

We both laughed.

In the middle of December, with temperatures in the twenties, Maureen and I broke the lease on our old apartment, infuriating our landlords, the Strafacis, and moved in immediately. I was in the middle of writing my first book, and its impending completion combined with the installment of my family in the new apartment to make me feel I had finally broken through into the world of adult accomplishment that for so many years had seemed just beyond my reach. It was nighttime, snowing and cold after I carried the last box up the stoop. We lit a fire in the fireplace and, with a bottle of French champagne my wife had selected, toasted our new home. Our daughter had just discovered that by going from the living room to the kitchen to the dining room and then out into the hallway and back to the living room she could complete a circle. She went round and round, and each time she passed us by, wearing her white ribbed sweater and tomato-red woolen tights and leather ankle boots, her expression combining intense focus with sheer glee, my wife and I chanted, "Here comes Jessica!" In the midst of this celebration smoke suddenly began to bil-

low out of the fireplace and into the room. We flapped at it and retreated coughing into the kitchen. It turned out that the flue was
badly constructed; wind gusting down the chimney caused the
smoke to back up, and so, although the fireplace was one of the
reasons we had been drawn to the apartment, we were never able
to use it.

Chapter 11

One of the many unexamined assumptions I had about marriage, in those early years of my own, was that it was a simple but rather inelastic proposition. We either adapted to its strictures or failed, and if we failed the marriage came to an end, either gradually or abruptly, and we disentangled ourselves as best we could and moved on. I had no idea then how adaptable marriage itself was, how pliable it could be, how it was possible to stretch and twist it to accommodate a bewilderingly diverse array of situations: the loveless marriage, the violent marriage, the companionate marriage, the marriage that represented a collusion of business interests. But as time passed and I saw the couples my wife and I had come to know trying to cope with the demands of living together and raising children, with professional disappointment and the relentless financial pressures, with the competition between their need to keep life interesting and to accept its limits and to give it value, I realized how improvisational marriage was. It was a notion, an air, the sketch for a blueprint of a house you would have to build yourself.

My first intimation of this fact came one Saturday morning a few months after we had moved into the brownstone. I was reading the papers at the kitchen table. I heard Maureen on the stairs; because the house was on a hillside and had settled, the stairs were out of plumb and groaned and squeaked with every step. A moment later she appeared in the doorway, a bulging plastic shopping bag in each hand, wearing the giddy look of someone in possession of a delicious secret.

"You won't believe what Syd just told me," she said.

"What?"

"He and Lois have an 'open marriage.' "

Syd and Lois Dubinsky lived across the street from us in a limestone house with a gargoyle set in the entablature; its stained eroding eyes seemed to be crying. We had met them through the Bialers and had become friends. That morning, Maureen had seen Syd out hosing down his sidewalk and, noticing that Lois wasn't around, had asked after her.

"She's gone to see her lover," Syd had said. He invited Maureen into the kitchen, where he explained their "open marriage."

Maureen had been dumbfounded and so was I. Syd and Lois were the last people we would have suspected of radical sexual experimentation. They were in their mid-forties and had been married for close to twenty years. Syd was a short, hirsute man who had grown up in a working-class Bronx neighborhood that was now a slum. He worked as a grievance representative for the hospital workers' union and had the braying voice and instinctively hectoring manner of someone who spends his days in hostile confrontations over trivial procedural issues. Lois was also short and sturdy and had grown up in the same Bronx neighborhood. She wore her dark hair cut short and said little. When she did speak, it was in a flat monotone. Her blunt, uninflected personality was such an unexpected but appropriate counterpoint to her husband's manic irrepressibility that it seemed an adaptive reaction.

Later that day, Syd stopped me outside the house. Having explained the situation to Maureen, he seemed to want to make sure I understood it as well, and we leaned against the wall with the carved lion's head to talk. Syd and Lois had two children, a teenage girl fighting a weight problem and a boy in the sixth grade I never saw without his skateboard. Both of them, Syd told me, knew about the open marriage. Neither he nor Lois believed in secrets and lies. An open marriage made sense for him and Lois, he said. Their relationship was based more on companionship than on passion. He was, he went on, attracted to a variety of women. Why should he deny his instincts? Why deprive himself of these experiences? To do so would have been in some profound way untrue to who he was. He had an obligation to himself to realize his nature.

The open marriage had been his idea; Lois had gone along somewhat reluctantly, he said. And the affairs had been largely his. But in the last couple of years she had taken a lover—an unemployed violinist who lived in New Orleans—and from time to time she flew down to spend weekends with him.

"We're all good friends," Syd added.

Syd was so insistent on this point—his complete lack of misgivings about his wife's affair—that I had the impression it wasn't really me he was trying to reassure; it was himself. My immediate reaction was disbelief, followed by scorn. Open marriages had, I thought, enjoyed a brief vogue fifteen years earlier but had then been discredited because, as those who experimented with them discovered, they generated precisely the kind of jealousy, mistrust, and rancor they were supposed to eradicate. But Syd, I could tell, was in earnest. He believed in marriage, saw himself as a responsible, reliable father to his children. He was trying to improvise within the form. That may have taken the shape of an alarming experiment, but there was no point in moralizing about it. Moralizing merely obscured a truth I began to grasp only that afternoon: in the time and place in which I lived, marriage lacked a governing superstructure. There were in fact no rules, no codified procedures. Each of us would have to figure out for ourselves what did and didn't work.

Chapter 12

Something went wrong with our marriage during those crucial first two years after our daughter was born. It was a gradual, imperceptible process—certainly nothing violent or dramatic happened—and we were, I think, scarcely aware of it at the time. In fact, while this was certainly one of the most important developments in my life, looking back now, I feel as if in some odd way I was absent when it occurred. There were the usual arguments and missed opportunities, but they add up to very little. I can't recall any specific scenes, any particular confrontations that even now, and much less at the time, illustrate the radical devolution that was taking place. It seems to have transpired largely offstage. But by the time we realized how far astray we had gone, it was too late, and we were never able to make it back.

I *was* aware that my wife had never quite reconciled herself to Brooklyn. Her life there contradicted her idea of herself. She was no longer the romantic nomad. She felt she had surrendered a crucial component of her identity. She was one of a generation of women who had absorbed the feminist assumptions of the seventies, had taken up a career only to find it ultimately unfulfilling, and so had given up the career to raise a child while her husband supported the family, but had then begun to resent the confinements in her new role. She felt, in Brooklyn, isolated, trapped, unappreciated, unchic.

It has often been asserted that the narrow roles imposed on women after World War II—when they were coerced out of their wartime jobs and into marrying young and raising families in suburbs of oppressive conformity—turned many of them into neurotics. This was no doubt true. But at least those women had the consolation of living in a society that sanctified the role of the mother. Their daughters, women like my wife, were becoming mothers at a time of profound uncertainty and raging disagreement about the roles they should adopt. The fact that they had so many more options than their mothers did forced them to make choices their mothers never had to make, and since the selection of any particular option ruled out the others, it left them with a gnawing sense of unfulfillment.

Women who had pursued careers instead of motherhood were desperate to have children. Longing choked them. Women who became mothers and continued to work were nagged with guilt about turning their children, during those early formative years, over to the nannies and au pairs and illegal aliens who collectively came to be known as caregivers. And women who gave up their careers to raise their children felt, first of all, that they had sacrificed the satisfaction, the prestige, and the power their careers had afforded them for domestic drudgery, and second, that in doing so they had become—particularly in a place like New York, where what you do determines who you are—less interesting, even less significant people. And they began to resent it.

I didn't realize to what extent resentment had begun to color my wife's view of our marriage until about four months after the baby was born. It was late on a Sunday afternoon. I had been working long hours at a new job, had gotten up on Saturday morning to do the grocery shopping and lug the enormous sack of all our dirty clothes to the laundry, and had played diligently with the baby.

"I'm going to go for a run," I announced.

"You can't go for a run," my wife said.

"What do you mean?"

"You have to look after the baby."

"I've been looking after her. I'm just going for a run, to get some exercise. I'll be back in fifty minutes."

"You're not going for a run. I've been in the house all week. I'm the one who needs a break."

"I worked all week, too."

"You go to an office. You don't think I know what you do there? I used to work in an office, too, remember? You sit around gossiping, you talk on the phone to friends, you read the paper, you go out to lunch, *while I'm here alone all day with the baby.*"

I looked at my wife in amazement. She was utterly serious and thoroughly enraged. *She hates her life,* I thought. I knew she felt confined and frustrated at times. But I had no idea then, despite minor outbursts over things like Sunday exercise, that she saw herself as the victim of a huge injustice, an injustice I had somehow perpetrated.

I understand now that a power shift in our marriage contributed to my wife's sense of frustration. When she stopped working, she had become dependent on me. I paid the bills and gave her the spending money she needed. Now she had to come to me for things. I tried not to lord it over her, tried to avoid acting like a tightwad, but when the overseas telephone calls became exorbitant or the credit-card charges got out of hand, I would sigh and mutter and sometimes complain, and this, after her life of complete independence, rankled her.

Furthermore, somewhat to my surprise, and to my wife's, my career had taken off. A week after getting a positive six-month review at the newsweekly and being made a permanent member of the staff, I quit. This perplexed and annoyed my editors, a congenial group of people, but I had decided at age twenty-eight that I wasn't cut out for life in a corporation. I never felt I belonged. I lacked the political instincts and the affability needed to thrive in a large group, which I suppose is another way of saying that I did, after all, have an "attitude."

Instead, through my wife I had gotten to know the editor of a small magazine that was just starting up and I joined the staff. Although it eventually folded, the magazine in its first few years succeeded beyond even our own expectations and I became known in the publishing world, not in any sense as a literary figure, merely as a capable journalist who could combine diligent reporting with occasionally interesting suppositions. Nonetheless, agents called wanting to represent me. I signed a book contract with a prestigious publisher. It was a period of deceptive flattery, of dangerously disproportionate self-regard, and I mention it only because it made my wife feel left behind, because I was rising in a world to which she felt she no longer belonged.

I sympathized. In bed at night, after my wife was asleep, I would enumerate the things I would give up in exchange for her health and wished I believed in an interventionist God with whom I could make the swap. But I also withdrew. I had an entirely separate life. It sometimes seemed like my real life, although of course it wasn't. And so, as did my wife, only for diametrically opposed reasons, I began to find our marriage a disappointment.

In those first few years we tried to talk. But those conversations almost invariably degenerated into bouts of complaining, and after a certain point—the point at which decorum is satisfied—

neither of us was interested in listening to the other's complaints. And so we talked less and less. We fell into the habit of withholding our feelings. While that ensured a surface civility, it also initiated the deceptiveness that eventually penetrated the very heart of the marriage.

Chapter 13

One night in the second year of our marriage, shortly after our ill-starred trip to Lone Mountain, I dreamed that my wife was drowning in a lake, and as she sank and struggled she called out, beseechingly at first, then hysterically, and then with rage, to a person on the deck of a nearby boat who was watching her drown and doing nothing to prevent it. That other person, I realized with a start that woke me up, was myself.

We had gone to Lone Mountain for my sister Amy's wedding. When my family lived abroad while I was growing up, we returned to the States (as we invariably referred to our country) every other summer on home leave, and almost every trip concluded with a family reunion in Lone Mountain. These reunions were massive affairs, more like clan gatherings, since most of my grandmother's nine brothers and sisters had children and grandchildren of their own. They drove in from Corbin, Kentucky, and Aiken, South Carolina, from Bryan, Ohio, and Gary, Indiana, and the old white farmhouse, where both my grandmother and my mother had been born, overflowed with as many as sixty people, the halls packed with their sleeping bags, the marble-topped sideboard in the dining room lined with smoked hams, bottles of Jim Beam and Old Grand-Dad, with tinfoil-covered mince pies, and plastic tubs of pimiento cheese and three-bean salad.

No one had lived in the house since my uncle Tip, a widower who lost a leg in a car accident, died in the late sixties. But most of the members of the clan still liked to visit, so the family had formed the Lone Mountain Corporation to collect dues for basic maintenance. This barely covered taxes and the fuel and phone bills. Any additional improvements to the house depended on whim. The cabinets we installed one summer in the kitchen came from a salvage center. In the late seventies someone bought a roll of suddenly unfashionable and therefore steeply discounted mustard-yellow shag carpet to cover the layers of worn linoleum in the dining room. Another year someone else arrived with a long marble bathroom countertop that had been discarded by a hotel during a renovation. We installed it in the upstairs hallway. Next to it we built a toilet, enclosed in flimsy Sheetrock, with only an old stained sheet for a door. These arrangements were haphazard and improvisational, but so were the reunions, so was the family.

At each gathering the house had first to be put in working order. The uncles, hard men whose mountain lineage showed in their narrow, carved faces and skeptical squints, worked as engineers, plant supervisors, farmers, and tractor salesmen, and they attended to the mechanics of the house. They cleaned out the gutters and caulked windows and reattached the drainpipes that had worked loose. They coaxed heat from the balky furnace, cleared the black snakes out from under the foundation, and, in a miracle of ingenuity, usually managed to start the old Model A, a rusting skeleton of a vehicle that lacked a chassis, utilized a pair of two-by-fours for bumpers, and sat for the rest of the year in the moldering doorless barn behind the house. Once these chores were completed, the uncles retired to the dining room, where they smoked Winstons and drank bourbon, played poker, argued politics, and provoked the younger and more liberal men present, like my father, by complaining about the "niggers."

The women cooked and cleaned in the kitchen and the younger ones complained that the men never did any housework, but the older ones, the aunts, neither expected the men to help out nor wanted them to since that would have offended *their* idea of manhood as well. The children, left to fend for themselves, had the most fun. We formed a large, inchoate pack, sometimes more than twenty or twenty-five of us, thundering through the parlor as the grown-ups protested and the screen door slammed in our wake, hiding in the smokehouse, intriguing in the rafters of the barn, roaming the wooded hills behind the house, visiting the general store, which still sold crackers in a barrel, following the railroad tracks to the trestle, where we jumped into the lake if the water was high enough, exploring the old mill with its supply of abandoned coffins, and camping out by the cemetery where our forebears were buried. My family never lived in Lone Mountain, but since we returned again and again, it had a permanence that all of the places we did live in lacked. It was as close as I ever got to home.

My sisters felt the same way. My sister Laurie was married there, and my sister Amy decided she would be too. She asked Maureen to be a bridesmaid and Jessica to be the flower girl. My wife had come to Lone Mountain once before for one of the family reunions. But she was not the type to throw herself into the fray and she had felt overwhelmed by the pandemonium generated by these loud Southerners, with their drunken opinion-mongering and raucous storytelling and affectionately obscene joking. The idea of returning to the place made her anxious, and she was also reluctant, for reasons she didn't explain, to participate in the wedding. Blind to the cause of her concerns, I talked her into ignoring them, but before we left, she told me, "I'm going to need extra attention."

"You've got it," I said.

The wedding took place in May. The dogwood flowers had faded by then, but the magnolias were still in bloom, and the cornflowers and rhododendrons, and the wild daylilies that grew in the ditches along the back roads, had just appeared. The days started cool, the roads and hollows wreathed in fog, and then warmed without becoming hot. Most of the clan had arrived the day before the wedding, and by that afternoon the kitchen and dining room of the old farmhouse were crowded and noisy.

It had rained heavily the previous month, and the ground was wet. We tried to prevent people from parking in the yard, where everyone always parked, because we planned to hold the party there and didn't want it churned to mud. My uncle Hobart made his appearance just in time for drinks. Several of us were sitting on the concrete porch as he drove up. Two of the younger boys ran out to wave him away from the yard, but he ignored them and pulled his big Oldsmobile onto the grass, spinning the wheels and creating wide muddy troughs as the car slithered from side to side.

Uncle Hobart lived in Roanoke, where he managed a par-three golf course he had built on land too hilly to farm. His life had not been uneventful. During World War II the B-17 he was flying had been shot down over Düsseldorf, and he had been taken prisoner by the Germans. He was a tall, stooped man who moved stiffly, as if his joints were permanently inflamed. His bony face was pale, but it had a red underglow, the choleric red of distemper. He was chronically irritable, proud, and angry. Other human beings incensed him, and he had on various occasions insulted a number of his own relatives so outrageously that they refused to speak to him for years. After the funeral service for one of his brothers, who had been cremated, he walked into the house and asked the grieving widow, "Why you keeping my brother in a jar?"

As a child I felt leery of Hobart, as if he might suddenly reach out and cuff me, and when I was grown up the residue of this unease remained. I never knew what might provoke him. But I liked his son Middler, who had arrived with him in the Oldsmobile. Middler, a couple of years older than me, was a quiet plump man with the flowing hair and mustache of a Restoration Cavalier. He worked as an electrician and lived in a trailer outside Roanoke that he had moved into after splitting up with his third wife. Middler had mysterious problems with the law. The year before the wedding, he and a friend had gone to collect some money from a third man, who pulled out a gun, killed the friend, and shot Middler in the stomach before fleeing. Middler had passed out, woken up, and dragged himself to a neighbor's house before he collapsed from lack of blood. He almost died in the hospital, where he stayed for three months. After he recovered he began dating Kate, his nurse, and she accompanied Middler and Hobart down to Lone Mountain.

Kate was tall and rawboned and had an ungainly manner. The tight, shiny red dress she wore for dinner that night exaggerated her figure. In fact, her entire character was a study in exaggeration. She found jokes funnier than they were and laughed in loud, hoarse sobs. She doted on the small children, and lavished extravagant praise on the food. She was excessively helpful; she jumped up from the dinner table to serve dishes as if she were the hostess. But her desire to be liked was so naked and endearing that everyone warmed to her. After dinner, she stood up, surveyed the room—the yellow walls with their topographical maps and amateurishly framed group photographs from reunions past, the rambunctious aunts and uncles and cousins all crowded around the various tables that had been shoved together to form one long banquet board—and hugged herself.

"I get such a special feeling about this place," she announced. "I'd like to come here and conceive a child."

Such moments made Lone Mountain, for me, the most completely realized spot on the earth. Unlike some of my cousins, who

considered the village squalid, who felt ashamed of it and congrat-
ulated themselves on having escaped into the enameled suburbs of
Houston or Jacksonville, I had always loved the place. And I had
loved the idea of my association with it as much as actually being
there. I loved the feeling of complete submersion that its commu-
nal life provided, the noise and tumult of the crowded rooms, the
palaver in the kitchen, even the long line for the bathroom in the
morning and the furious cursing that arose from inside when, inevitably, the hot water ran out. And I loved the people, despite
their prejudices and idiosyncrasies: the chain-smoking uncles who
considered themselves yellow-dog Democrats but who had despised every Democratic presidential candidate since Harry Tru-
man; the aunts, with their ability to manufacture a crisis from
something as mundane as mismatched tablecloths; the teenagers
who, wrapped in blankets, could mysteriously remain asleep on
the living room floor until noon despite the clamor around them.
They had a vividness and specificity you didn't find among the cen-
sored personalities in the big northeast cities. I hoped, as we prepared for the wedding the following day, that my wife was
responding to all this as I was, that if she didn't experience the
urge to conceive a child in Lone Mountain, she would at least, like
Kate, get a special feeling for the place.

The wedding was scheduled for early afternoon. It took
place in the same church my mother had attended as a child, which
was also the church where the funeral service for my grandfather
Cawood had been held. The church was a small stone building
with a nave that sloped down toward the altar, behind which, hidden by a purple velvet curtain, stood a large tank for full-
immersion baptisms. When the pews were full, the guests sitting
in an expectant hush, the bridesmaids filed out and took their positions to the left of the altar. Maureen was among them. They all
wore long, flowered dresses and carried bouquets. Anxiety exac-
erbated the tremor in Maureen's arm, and in that quiet moment

before the organist began the bridal march, that moment of coughing and rustling when everyone's eyes were on the bridesmaids, the bouquet she was carrying shook visibly. It was only then that I understood why she had been reluctant to play a part in the ceremony. Her role was unessential, she could have easily begged off, but I had talked her into it.

Maureen had adapted to her condition by trying for the most part to pretend that it didn't exist, and she counted on those around her to do the same. I was sitting in the first row, and I knew that at that moment she wanted to run from the room or sink through the floor, that she hated herself for agreeing to be a member of the wedding, that she would have given almost anything to be almost anywhere else. But there was nothing she, or I, could do.

Then the music started, and the guests in unison swiveled their heads to watch my sister Amy, escorted by my father, enter the church. My two-year-old daughter, the flower girl, preceded her. Jessica's expression was solemn. She wore a high-waisted white dress and carried a woven basket filled with rose petals, which she was supposed to scatter in Amy's path. But she forgot this assignment until she reached the front of the church, at which point, realizing her mistake and determined to correct it, she up-ended the basket and dumped all the petals on the floor. A murmur of laughter swept through the front of the church, and my daughter, thinking she was being praised, smiled happily.

When the ceremony was over I waited for Maureen, and we walked together out of the church. The guests milled about on the sun-dappled driveway in festive aimlessness, waiting to toss rice at Amy and her new husband when they emerged. Uncle Hobart approached us stiffly out of the crowd. He wore a black suit and a fedora. He seemed funereal and ominous—a specter haunting the joyous ceremony. I introduced him to Maureen. His pale eyes glittered behind his glasses as he sized her up. He took her hand to shake it, then gripped it tightly, almost harshly, and looked down at it.

"Everybody in the church could see that arm of yours shaking," he said. "It's a shame there's not a damn thing you can do about it."

He turned and walked away. Maureen was stunned, rendered speechless for a moment by this vicious, gratuitously inflicted cruelty, then her eyes filled with tears.

"Why did he say such an awful thing?" she asked.

I shook my head. I felt as shocked and dismayed as my wife. The conception I had of our family—as life's one true haven, a place where we would all look out for one another's best interests, where we would all protect one another—had been violated, betrayed, and the urge to strike my uncle across his face seized me. That was of course out of the question. He was an old man, after all, and my grandmother's brother. I told Maureen that he was bitter and spiteful and that, like everyone else in the family whom he had insulted, we should simply ignore him. But my uncle hadn't merely insulted my wife, he had wounded her, and far too deeply for her to be able to disregard him.

"I knew I shouldn't have come," she said. "You were supposed to give me extra attention. You were supposed to protect me."

If I felt I had been betrayed by my uncle, she felt, I saw, that she had been betrayed by me. And in a way she was right. I *had* betrayed her. I was the one who had talked her into ignoring her doubts about becoming a bridesmaid. If she had followed her own instincts, she would have declined to participate. I was only trying to do good, but that hardly exonerated me; so much of the harm we do to others comes from our attempts to help them.

"I'm never coming back," she said.

She never did. From then on, I went to the Lone Mountain gatherings without her.

Chapter 14

*Cheating in a marriage is one of those acts that, like committing sui-*cide or appearing naked in public, at first seem freighted with an insurmountable taboo. For most of us, it requires the first time out an extraordinary effort of will, for it means that we pass a divide, that we cast off a version of ourselves in which we thought we believed and substitute for it one we consider distasteful, disappointing, degrading, even abhorrent. Even if, usually by convincing ourselves we are the victim of one breach or another, we muster the strength to violate our promises, most of us think we will never be able to get away with it. Something—the smell of the lover, suspiciously excessive affection when returning home from a late evening at the office, the simple but unmistakable aura of guilt—will give us away. But it almost never does. Our husbands, our wives, remain innocent, encased in their obliviousness as tightly as we, the cheaters, are in our lies, and a close imitation of the life we had been living before proceeds.

I met Alex Carras in the expense-account world of polished mahogany and crisp linen, muted voices and mineral water, leather-jacketed wine lists and carbon-smudged credit-card receipts. My first book had been published around that time to largely positive and at times even enthusiastic reviews. I had left the small magazine I helped start and had a new, slightly more lucrative contract with an established publication. Editors at other magazines asked me to write reviews, travel articles, and, from time to time, those sycophantic but highly remunerative profiles of interior designers that appear in the "shelter books." My success, modest as it was, astonished me. I was earning a living not just as a journalist but as a writer. Some of the work was mercenary and intellectually suspect, but I enjoyed it nonetheless. I thought of myself as operating in the tradition of Samuel Johnson, and I liked to quote his line to the effect that anyone who doesn't write for money is a fool. My life, I felt, was beginning to take shape.

Business brought Alex and me together, first over lunch—someone had suggested I contact her for a project I was working on—and then a second time, for dinner. She was an entrancing woman. Her black hair hung in a thick glossy sheet almost to her waist. She had liquid black eyes, olive skin, and an Indian-like indentation in the bridge of her nose that was visible only in profile. Her smile revealed perfect white teeth and tugged the skin at the corners of her eyes into a fan of tiny creases. Her movements formed a complicated and precise choreography. That first meal was at an Italian restaurant. Alex ordered linguine, and before each bite she used one hand to flip back her luxuriant hair, then patiently twirled her pasta onto her fork, daubing the tips of the spooled noodles with a piece of bread to soak up the excess sauce and avoid a dribbled stain on her white satin blouse. Replacing the fork on her plate, she lifted her wineglass, keeping her eyes on me while she sipped.

She was in sales. Accustomed to thinking, as journalists did, of salespeople as swindlers and opportunists, I was surprised to find that Alex was a genuine idealist. Belief in what she was selling was essential for her. Cynicism, I saw as she described the grueling daily rejection she had to endure and the alchemical tricks with which she sustained an optimistic frame of mind, had no place in her world. I was intrigued. Her work in sales, like the indented bridge of her nose, gave her an exotic cast. It declared that she was the product of a foreign culture.

She had grown up in Queens, as the youngest of nine children, she said as I ordered a second bottle of wine during our second meal. Both her parents were from the Greek island of Mykonos. Her father had worked as a mechanic in the subway yards until he died of liver failure at the age of fifty-three. She never attended college, living instead a wild life among the dissolute rich on the Mediterranean and in Miami. Various older men—arms dealers, ivory exporters, liquor-store owners—supported her. She spent her days beside their pools and on the decks of their yachts. After a few narrow escapes—a motorcycle accident she walked away from that broke the neck of the man who'd been driving, an orgy in Marseille that ended when one of the girls suffered a cocaine-induced seizure and died—she'd settled down and eventually married the man who'd gotten her into sales, where her career was flourishing.

This background entranced me as much as did her white smile and her dexterity with a fork. I admired the fact that she had pulled herself up out of that impoverished background, had escaped intact from her period of dissolute glamour on Mediterranean yachts, and, without even the benefit of a college education, had elbowed her way up into the upper levels of her field, and now confidently wielded a gold-plated corporate charge card to pay for hundred-dollar dinners in Italian restaurants.

By the end of that second meal, our conversation had become confiding and suggestive. We talked, with dangerous candor, about our marriages. Her husband, Alex said, was considerate, gentle, successful in his chosen field, socially connected—a man, in other words, with a number of desirable traits—but like the men who had provided for her during her wild days, he was older. He had one child from his previous marriage and felt disinclined to have another. In addition, she found him emotionally inarticulate. For some reason so profoundly intuitive she had difficulty explaining it, she could no longer bear sleeping with him. The chasm of sexual possibility suddenly yawned before us.

After dinner I escorted her to the curb. The restaurant was downtown, near the waterfront, and an autumn wind swept off the harbor, chilling the wet air. Cars rattled along the dark, cobblestoned street, their bouncing headlights briefly illuminating the steam that swirled from a manhole and was scattered by the wind. Alex wore a billowing taupe raincoat tied with a sash and carried an oversized black portfolio case so thin it seemed two-dimensional. She raised her hand in a beckoning gesture both peremptory and graceful. A taxi instantly shrieked to a halt; it was as if she had the powers of a witch.

We kissed, briefly, on the lips. It was almost ostentatiously perfunctory, that overcivilized Continental kiss, but we both knew that this was a pretense, and when we got together for a third time, at yet another exorbitantly priced restaurant, Alex reached across the table and began to stroke my hands even before the food arrived. Her husband, she explained, was out of town. We left quickly—this bill also went on the expense account—and took a taxi back to her apartment.

The illicit nature of what we were doing thrilled us both. Adultery—*an affair*—seemed rakish, glamorous. It promised, on that cab ride through the cold November night to Alex's apartment, to infuse our lives with drama and intrigue and even danger. We did not at that time discuss the danger, but we each thought about it. We believed then that the danger lay in the risk of discovery. But it wasn't just our marriages that we were jeopardizing, though we

realized this only later; it was our sense of our selves. We had become—if we weren't going to confess to our spouses, and neither
of us had the slightest intention of doing that—liars.

We had to justify this to ourselves; we knew that even then,
of course, but at the time that had seemed easy. We had laid the
groundwork for the process in those first conversations about our
discontent with our marriages. I felt unappreciated at home and
was now acting on an attraction to someone who did appreciate
me. Was that so immoral? Alex, for her part, had a rationalization
so convenient, so reassuring—her husband didn't want her to
have a child—that it essentially served as a license to cheat.

And anyway, I thought later that night, alone in the cab taking me back to Brooklyn, wasn't there something overrefined
about the moral squeamishness I was experiencing? As long as I
shouldered my responsibilities to my wife and daughter, why
shouldn't I do what I wanted to do? I wouldn't be the first. As the
cab crossed the Brooklyn Bridge, passed the women's jail with its
bleakly lit glass-brick windows, and turned onto Atlantic Avenue,
I made a mental list of some of the members of the club I had just
joined. Franklin Roosevelt, Dwight Eisenhower, Martin Luther
King, Jr., John Kennedy, Ernest Hemingway, F. Scott Fitzgerald,
Pablo Picasso, William Faulkner, Lord Horatio Nelson, William
Paley, Peter the Great, William Randolph Hearst, John Updike,
Jerzy Kosinski, John Huston, Chiang Kai-shek, Ben Bradlee, network news anchors, celebrated Yale professors, Nobel Prize–
winning doctors, senators and governors, admirals and priests,
and women also, Churchill's mother, Churchill's wife, Churchill's
daughter-in-law, to mention merely one distinguished family—
they had all committed adultery. None of them seemed morally
stigmatized. You could almost call it a mark of distinction.

Reassured, I let myself into our dark apartment. The humming refrigerator made the only noise. The long-haired cat we had
recently acquired—and that my daughter had named Ariel after

the girl in *The Little Mermaid* but ended up calling Cooch—
brushed against my leg. Maureen was asleep and, of course, so too
was Jessica. Two dreaming females, each alone in a quiet room. I
stopped at my daughter's door, then went in and sat down next to
her. At that moment the reassurance I had conjured up in the cab
drained out of me so quickly I was left light-headed, almost ill. I
had betrayed not just my wife but also my daughter. I felt dishonest, caddish, corrupt. I wanted to lie beside her, to steal some consolation and encouragement from her, a foretaste of what I hoped
she would bring me in old age, but I couldn't bring myself to do it.
My daughter shifted in her sleep, murmuring something about a
swing, and her bed squeaked. We had recently replaced her crib
with a twin bed made of three-sided red and blue pipes; they
squeaked because I had bolted them together improperly. I was
doing as bad a job of keeping our family intact as I had done of as-
sembling that bed, failing as a husband and father as well as a
handyman. It all, I saw, could very easily come unscrewed.

Chapter 15

*I*s life the pursuit of a moral definition of the self? Or is that just a literary device, the motive for the modern protagonist? I had always
had my suspicions, especially since the people who proclaim such
an undertaking as our one authentic existential occupation—
Philip Roth, if you believe Claire Bloom's memoir; Sigmund
Freud, if you accept Jeffrey Masson's scholarship; Bruno Bettel-
heim, according to one biographer—often prove to be the most
dishonest, manipulative, and deluded among us.

In any event, I never developed the habit of honesty. Honesty
requires hard work. It is easier just to tell people what would
please them. As complications branched out in my life, as my approach to my marriage became more dutiful and formal, I decided
that the theory of the unified personality was a fiction. I subscribed instead to the Japanese theory of the masks of life: the
mask of the father, the mask of the husband, the mask of the employee. I didn't see the need to lead an integrated life. It was a self-
serving approach; it allowed me to treat my dishonesty as
functional, an adaptive strategy devoid of a moral dimension.

But I also felt that it was truer to human experience. Our
real life is our interior one. We're imprisoned in a subjectivity that
even the most articulate among us can never fully communicate.

No one is completely open with anyone else. We would destroy one another if we were. We all determine not only the degree of personal dishonesty we can tolerate but the degree of candor those around us can withstand.

Alex and I worked in offices near enough to each other that we could get together for lunch or midafternoon coffee—meetings that often led to fevered carnal gropes in the fire stairwells of nearby hotels or the backseats of cabs if the Plexiglas partition was sufficiently knicked and scarred to prevent the driver from watching through the rearview mirror. We felt and acted like teenagers in a constant state of unappeasable overstimulation.

From time to time we rented hotel rooms that management slyly offered guests who promised to vacate by three, but even with the half-day discount rates—the hot-sheets special—this began to get expensive. After nine months of this we found a tiny studio in an inconspicuous neighborhood. I bought a futon and a portable radio. Alex contributed beeswax candles, a knotted throw rug, and two expensive crystal wineglasses as oversized and as fragile as human egos. The partially furnished room corresponded to the uncompleted personal evolution that had made the affair possible. But evolution was proceeding. Which was why, when we met there once a week or so, after making love and fixing dinner, we increasingly argued.

While I never overcame my guilt about the affair, Alex conducted it with the moral vigor of a crusade. She had begun it in part as a way of punishing her husband for preventing her from having the sort of life to which she felt entitled. At first, she'd had no further objective.

"It's a good thing I don't want to marry you," she told me once during those early days, "because if I did I'd steal you from your wife. I could, you know. I've stolen other men away from women."

"I don't doubt it," I said, and we both laughed nervously.

But Alex was, as she described herself, "goal-oriented." She believed you gave your life meaning and shape, and took control of it by identifying goals and pursuing them relentlessly. And so her rationalization of the affair as reactive—retribution against her husband—soon came to seem to her unsatisfactory. She began to think of it then as a way of precipitating a crisis in her marriage, and finally as a way out of her marriage. Eventually, as the evolution in her thinking continued, she decided she did want to marry me. We both should leave our spouses, she declared in the same tone of moral conviction she used in sales presentations; it was what was right. When I replied that I wasn't so sure, she said the time had come to discuss the entire matter with Sharon.

Sharon was her therapist. Alex valued Sharon's opinion as if she were family, which in a way she was, and Sharon seemed full of opinions, which Alex passed on to me, opinions about Alex and her husband, about me and my wife, about Alex's parents. At one point I told Alex I thought psychologists were not supposed to give patients their opinions, that the point of therapy was for the patient to discover her own solutions. "That's what she did at first," Alex said. "She wouldn't say anything, or she would ask me, 'Why do you say that?' But after a while I told her that wasn't the kind of relationship I wanted. I wanted feedback. I wanted conversation. I wanted to feel that we were friends. And so she changed."

Sharon's professional flexibility suggested to me that she was, probably for financial reasons, more interested in appeasing her patients than in challenging them. Still, that didn't mean she was necessarily a fraud. Ridiculing city dwellers and their therapists is so easy it has become a literary and cinematic convention. But the city can be a grueling, desolate place, where genuine friendships are hard to come by and more difficult to sustain. Why not procure the understanding of a therapist? A therapist, like the members of your family, has to accept you for who you are. So I didn't consider Alex's dependence on Sharon to be comical or sad and I didn't mind meeting Sharon. I had a lot of shortcomings as a human being, but I thought I understood myself. I felt I could make a pretty good case for why I was who I was and why I did what I did.

One afternoon the following week we took a taxi up to Sharon's office. It was raining and cold; we both wore coats and carried umbrellas. Sharon worked out of a suite of doctors' offices in a prewar limestone co-op. The suite had its own entrance, down from the building's main brass doors, which were protected by a royal-blue canopy and guarded by a uniformed doorman who studied us with open curiosity as soon as he saw where we were headed.

Alex rang the bell and shouted, "It's me," into the intercom. The lock buzzed and clicked, and we descended several steps into a tiny, bare foyer. Three identical white doors faced us. Behind the nearest we could hear the muted sobbing of a patient. The middle door opened. A short, round woman in a violet caftan beckoned us in. The office was nondescript; two chairs, a couch, a Mondrian print. A rain-spattered window at sidewalk level provided a view of the legs and boots and swinging umbrella tips of passing pedestrians.

Alex made introductions and hung our coats and scarves in the closet. She was talking with the exaggerated animation of a hostess afraid that at any moment the conversation might falter. Alex and I sat down on the couch. Sharon settled into one of the chairs, rested her chin on her hand, and studied me with crafty eyes and a conspiratorial smile.

Alex turned to me. "Why are you nervous?" she asked.

"I'm not nervous."

"Yes, you are."

"No, I'm not."

"He's not nervous," Sharon said to Alex. "You're nervous."

"I'm not nervous," Alex protested.

Sharon and I shared a look, a brief but knowing look. I sensed, to my surprise, a potential ally.

"So tell me about yourself, John," Sharon said.

Psychologists, like teachers, favor those with the answers and I had all the answers. My wife and I were no longer in love, I explained, but she was chronically ill and we had a child. I had met Alex, we were attracted to each other. Stronger feelings arose from this attraction. Eventually, after a lot of hesitation and misgivings, we had begun an affair. Now, I told the therapist, I felt I had three options. One, I could leave my wife and child. Two, I could stay with my wife and stop seeing Alex. Three, I could stay with my wife and continue to see Alex. I didn't want to leave my wife and child, I said. I felt I had a duty to support them, particularly in light of my wife's condition. On the other hand, I didn't see the point of remaining faithful. In a loveless marriage it seemed an exercise in futility. Why deprive myself of some degree of joy, delight, and intimacy? So I would honor my duty to my wife but allow myself this involvement with someone who meant a great deal to me. It's a compromise, I said, but it seems to be what's best for everyone.

Sharon nodded. "You seem to have thought it through pretty carefully," she said.

I shrugged. It was all too pat, too tidy, it was intellectualized and self-serving. I knew that even then. But I was performing for the therapist, trying to impress her, hoping to solidify our nascent alliance.

"What about *my* needs?" Alex asked. "What about me?"

"Well," Sharon said, "John's determined what his needs are and what he can and can't do about them. You have to do the same."

Alex tossed her hair back. It was the same spirited gesture that had tantalized me when we first met. She looked at her therapist and then at me. Anger flared in her dark eyes. This was not what she had wanted to hear. I shrugged again, this time apologetically. While there was nothing dishonest in any of what I had said I nonetheless felt as if I was perpetrating a fraud. I had co-opted Alex's therapist.

Chapter 16

That summer I had earned some extra money, so my wife and I took Jessica on vacation to Corsica. We chose Corsica because Ian Braudel, my wife's former boyfriend, would be there with his girlfriend, Geneviève, and her five-year-old daughter, Ichelle. Ian was British, but he lived in Paris, where he worked as a curator for the Musée des Beaux Arts. Fifteen years earlier, when they both first moved to Paris, he and Maureen had lived together in a one-room flat behind the Hôtel des Invalides. He had owned a motorcycle back then, and I had this image of Maureen sitting behind him in a red leather jacket from the period that she still owned, clutching his waist as he roared through the narrow Paris streets. Neither had been interested in settling down at the time, and had gone their separate ways. But while their involvement ended, they had always remained friends, and I felt that in some ways Maureen's relationship with Ian was deeper, truer, and possibly more enduring than her relationship with me. The thought didn't make me jealous. Neither did the fact that, whenever she visited Paris, Maureen stayed in his apartment, a rambling place, with rippling parquet floors and a dusty gilded ceiling, in an eighteenth-century building at the foot of Montmartre.

In Corsica we rented a yellow stone house in a walled medieval village high in the mountains. The rooftop terrace looked out over the harsh stony slopes down to the ocean. Each morning Jessica and I walked across the cobblestoned village square to its single shop, where, for breakfast, we bought fresh bread and tiny, fragrant peaches from a loquacious woman with a mustache who wore a formless black shift and, like all Corsicans, seemed more Italian than French. Afterward, we drove down to the beach, a sweep of white sand that swung around a turquoise cove. Most of the women were topless and many of the sunbathers wore nothing. Entire families of French bourgeoisie—the bearded father, the ample-hipped mother, the sleek teenage son, and the nubile daughter—splashed nude in the surf. It was, for someone from America, a startlingly pagan display, and it made me aware of how often morality is really a question of custom.

Ian and Geneviève and Ichelle had rented a house in a village a short drive from ours, and we usually met them at the beach. Jessica had turned three that spring. No longer a toddler, she was now a child, independent, curious, with sturdy legs and blond hair that the Mediterranean sun further lightened. Despite the language barrier, lowered somewhat because of Ichelle's exposure to American cartoons, the two girls played together happily, improvising in sign language whenever a more complex idea needed to be communicated. Ichelle showed Jessica how to run a tab, for which her parents had to pay, from the Corsican who ran the drinks stand at the end of the beach, and the two of them, in complete surrender to the temptation of consumer credit, were rarely without small bulb-shaped bottles of Orangina in their hands.

We adults would read on the sand through the morning. For lunch we walked up to a restaurant overlooking the beach. All the tables were outside, on a stone patio. Loosely woven mats strung between poles provided a latticed shade. We ate salads, squid grilled in oil, and french fries sprinkled with vinegar, and drank a freshly pressed rosé from a vineyard a few miles away. In the evening, sunburned and salt-encrusted, we drove back up to the village. After showering, Ian and Geneviève and Ichelle would come over, and for dinner we would cook mysterious species of Mediterranean fish we bought at the market near the beach.

When I think back to Corsica, I remember the stony mountains and the brilliant sea and the polished blues of the sky, but I also recall a creeping sensation of emptiness. Throughout our idyll there, Maureen and I were pretending to enjoy each other's company. Things had turned bad with extraordinary quickness; eighteen months was all, and nothing truly monstrous had occurred during that time. A few arguments, a few grievances that went unaddressed, a sulky mutual withdrawal, and suddenly we found that the air had been sucked out of the marriage. We slept side by side but rarely touched. Jessica became all the more important to us. She provided us with the excuse and the opportunity to talk. She was all we shared, and if she wasn't around we had nothing to say to each other.

We had both been aware of this situation but obliquely. It was embedded in the routine of our lives, which made it, if not unnoticeable, at least easy to avoid. In Corsica, with its dazzling light and punishing heat, its salt and sand and casual nudity and freshly pressed rosé wine, we were forced by the contrast to recognize how thoroughly cold the marriage had become. I realized for the first time that I had no idea why I had gotten married. The commitment it required was so absolute. It allowed for no ambivalence, and in Corsica I saw I had become so ambivalent about everything that I felt almost paralyzed.

That was why the relationship between Ian and Geneviève fascinated me. I had considered ambivalence—a fluctuation between one thing and its opposite, the simultaneous experience of attraction and repulsion—to be a sign of weak character. It was, if not a mental defect, a representation of anxiety. We should aspire to decisiveness, I had believed, we should seek to know our own minds, and then we should seek resolution in all our affairs. But Ian and Geneviève were a virtual case study in ambivalence; they had incorporated it into the very structure of their lives.

Geneviève had short, dark hair and a small perfect face, and she dressed in the effortlessly impeccable style of the Parisian woman. She was a radiologist at the American Hospital, and her manner was reserved and serious, almost grave. She was married to an EEC economist, her daughter's father, and she and her daughter would spend two or three weeks with him and then two or three weeks with Ian, in the dusty, gilded apartment at the foot of Montmartre. Ichelle had her own room there, a lonely room at the end of a long hall, its closet filled with a heap of plastic Barbies. She and her mother kept clothes, toiletries, books, and photographs in each place.

It was, to a provincial American like myself, incomprehensible. How could a mother let her child grow up with two fathers? Why would one woman want the strain of managing two households? Why would two men in their mid-forties who had other options be willing to share one woman, regardless of how extraordinary she was? How could three adults accept such an unresolved state of affairs?

However, they all apparently found the arrangement convenient. The men enjoyed Geneviève's companionship but also wanted a degree of freedom. Geneviève was able to avoid having to choose between them, which would have meant giving up one of them. They lived in a fluid environment largely devoid of expectations. They made Americans—with their schematic approach to their own interests, their relentless pursuit of clearly defined goals—seem mechanical and inflexible.

Alex was in that respect prototypically American. She had a passionate and I thought admirable desire for moral clarification. At the same time she had freighted her life with such ardently held but narrowly focused expectations that I felt sure she was setting herself up for disappointment. Why did we in America have this conviction that life could only be redeemed by total commitment to another person? Such a belief seemed——that summer in Corsica, as I observed the courteous formality with which Ian and Geneviève behaved toward each other——to be a sort of vestigial utopianism, a relic of the Puritan dream of perfect harmony. I began to think that the American desire for moral resolution, our aversion to ambivalence, was, like our discomfort with nudity, merely a question of custom.

Chapter 17

In his massive work, Family, Sex, Marriage, the social historian Lawrence Stone observes that in certain prominent cities during the 1600s, at least one of the partners in one third of all marriages had been married before. "This means that in the seventeenth century the remarriage rate, made possible by death, was not far off that in our own day, made possible by divorce," Stone writes. "In both periods consecutive legal polygamy has been extremely common. . . . Indeed, it looks very much as if modern divorce is little more than a functional substitute for death. The decline of the adult mortality rate after the late eighteenth century, by prolonging the expected duration of marriage to unprecedented lengths, eventually forced Western society to adopt the institutional escape of divorce."

Consecutive polygamy. The phrase, I thought when I came across the book the year we went to Corsica, had a nonjudgmental, bracingly anthropological ring. It made the rationalists of the Enlightenment and the moralistic Victorian bourgeoisie appear to be in fact the practitioners of a particularly devious form of paganism. They were consecutive polygamists. Furthermore, Stone's observation suggested that for those of us alive in the late-twentieth century, the constraints of monogamy were without historical precedent.

In the fall, Alex began to find it difficult to sustain the contradictions the affair had created in her life. To force the situation, she began leaving clues for her husband, dropping hints that something was amiss. She told me she often talked to him about me, but that she had described us as "friends." She said one day she had called him by my name. When we went skiing just before Christmas, she told him that she was going with a group of friends, and that I was among the group. As time went by these hints—as she reported them to me, without ever describing them as hints—became less oblique, more provocative and daring. When I was away on an extended business trip, she telephoned me every morning from her apartment, and a month later, after her husband opened the bill, had trouble explaining the unprecedented series of calls to San Francisco, Seattle, Dallas, Salt Lake City. She seemed to want to taunt her husband, as if, having had an affair to punish him for refusing to allow her to have a child, she now had the desire to punish him further for unwittingly forcing her to be unfaithful.

Finally, she decided to accompany me on another business trip, this one to Los Angeles. I thought this might be unwise, but she insisted. She would tell her husband, she said, that she was going to visit an old school friend. As the date of departure drew near, she told me that she had revealed to her husband that it was me with whom she would be traveling and even that she was going to be staying in my hotel room. But, she said she told him, he had no cause for alarm—this was only to save money; she and I were, after all, just friends. As a final precipitating device, she demanded that I pick her up at her apartment for the drive to the airport.

"Is Tom going to be there?" I asked. I had never met Tom, but from everything I had heard, and not just from Alex, he was a generous and gracious, eminently likable man, the sort of man I would have enjoyed having for a friend.

"Maybe," she said.

"Forget it," I said. "You can take a cab to the airport."

"I don't see what's the problem," she said. "He already knows we're going on the trip together."

"You're rubbing his face in it."

"No I'm not. And if you didn't pick me up, he might get suspicious."

"Oh, come on."

"He might think you weren't really going with me, that I was using you as a cover for a trip I was taking with someone else."

"Lex . . ."

"Anyway, he said he wants to meet you."

The day we were scheduled to leave was one of the first warm days of April. It was excessively, unwholesomely warm, I felt. I wanted a chilling rain, a blanketing fog. I drove into the city weighted down with the certainty of impending confrontation, a conscript in a battle whose cause had no claim on me. What did Alex hope to accomplish? Did she want to place the two men in her life side by side for the sake of comparison? Did she hope to provoke a showdown? Did she expect me, once I'd come face-to-face with her husband, to understand what she was forced to endure and rescue her? Did she expect her husband, when confronted with her lover, to perceive the jeopardy into which his marriage had fallen and to take whatever extreme measures were needed to win back her love? Why had she orchestrated this melodrama? Why had I allowed myself to be manipulated into participating in this exercise in humiliation?

I parked in front of a hydrant just beyond Alex's building, a small Art Deco office tower that had been converted into apartments. The security guard in her lobby was watching, appropriately, a soap opera on a small black-and-white television—or maybe it was the video monitor for the security cameras, maybe I only thought it would have been appropriate for him to be watching a soap opera. Anyway, I asked him to let her know I was downstairs and went back out to the street to make sure my car wasn't being ticketed. A few minutes later Alex and Tom came through the door. Tom was silver-haired, with gentle eyes and a strong chin. He wore a black T-shirt and baggy corduroy trousers, and he carried Alex's leather traveling bag in one hand. They squinted for a moment in the hard spring light and then saw me. Alex waved girlishly. Tom broke into an embarrassed grin. I felt the same rictus of a smile distort my face. Alex introduced us.

"At long last we meet," Tom said.

He reached for my hand and shook it methodically, with a practiced and diplomatic finesse. I detected no rage, no coiled tension. Everything about him was measured, almost slow, as if he were moving through water.

"Alex's told me so much about you," he said.

I uttered some platitudes and looked at Alex, who gave me a tight, defiant smile. Tom stowed her bag in my trunk.

"Have fun in L.A., guys," he said. When he shook my hand a second time his expression altered for a moment and I caught a glimpse far back in his eyes of a quiet resignation that shook me more deeply than any anger he might have shown. He turned and walked in his tempered, careful way back into the building.

"Why did you do this?" I said as I got in the car.

"Do what?" Alex asked. "Do what?"

The trip to Los Angeles accomplished the objective Alex had set for it. Shortly after we returned, she called me at work and announced, in what I couldn't help interpreting as a tone of triumph, "We're separating."

A friend of Tom's, she said, had convinced him that no wife flies off to California with another married man unless she is having an affair with him. Tom had not actually confronted Alex—confrontation was alien to his nature—but the night before, he had in his gentle way wondered aloud if something was going on and she had—gladly, eagerly—seized the opportunity to confess. There was no violence or anger, she reported. Instead, a long, productive, "heartfelt" conversation had ensued, a conversation that made her feel closer to her husband than she had in years.

They both agreed it wasn't working out, though Tom declared that he loved Alex and wanted to stay together, and sounded, as Alex reported it to me anyway, baffled about precisely how he had failed as a husband. Nonetheless, when she persisted, he proved, in accordance with his reputation, astonishingly, even excessively generous. He moved in with the friend who had convinced him his wife was betraying him and allowed Alex to stay in the apartment (a sleek modern place with huge windows, gleaming pine floorboards, and tubular Wassily chairs) while he continued to pay the mortgage. He suggested she spend alternate weekends at the summerhouse they had just rented, with his money, and use his new gunmetal-gray Saab to get there and back. He offered her a handsome financial settlement.

Tom seemed, in fact, so noble in defeat that it made me wonder again why Alex was leaving him. What had the guy done wrong? He may have been "emotionally inarticulate," as she had said, but was that such a crime? He was solid, reliable, considerate. The fact that he expressed his feelings through devotion instead of language, steadfast behavior rather than grand romantic gestures, probably made them more trustworthy. I wondered if Alex was making a mistake. When she called me that day after the trip to Los Angeles to announce their separation, I had started to discourage her from doing anything rash and she had become irate.

She had no reservations. She was excited, even jubilant, in those first few weeks following their decision. She felt that her life, after several stalled years, was moving forward again. Possibilities bloomed.

Chapter 18

Maureen's medical condition had worsened, noticeably if not dramatically. She had spent the better part of a year in search of a doctor who would say that what she suffered from was not Parkinson's disease. She had tried a cruelly rigorous yeast-free diet to no avail. She had seen an allergist who sold her a shoeboxful of bottles whose various inky fluids she was supposed to mix in a complex formula of droplets three times a day and consume with water. It didn't work, either. She tried a physical therapist and an orthopedic doctor who suggested an elaborate series of useless exercises. Finally, she ended up with a prominent neurologist at Columbia Presbyterian who persuaded her to accept that what she had was in fact Parkinson's disease. He prescribed Sinemet, which quickly alleviated her symptoms but left her with chronic insomnia. By the time I got home for dinner she often felt exhausted. The day had passed when she could push a stroller with a baby in it for eight miles.

Maureen's illness was, of course, unfair—unfair to me, to our daughter, but most of all to Maureen herself. Any feelings of bitterness I had about our situation were shamefully irrelevant. They paled into invisibility next to the understandable and complicated mixture of embarrassment, outrage, despair, and guilt that Maureen, despite her relative success in viewing things philosophically, still from time to time experienced. I was the healthy one, the lucky one. It was up to me to do everything I could to help her deal with her condition. That was my duty.

Until Maureen became ill, I'd never had much reason to think about the notion of "duty." Who did? Beyond mundane concerns like paying bills, filing tax returns, and voting, duty had no bearing on my life or the lives of most of the people I knew. True duty, duty that required sacrifice, that required you to set aside what was in your own interest for a greater good, had never become an issue in our times. We had no war, no stirring political crisis; American troops had pulled out of Vietnam by the time we graduated from high school. Duty was, if anything, regarded as vaguely provincial, increasingly obsolete, and even somehow suspect. To invoke duty suggested that you hadn't thought the matter through. After all, what was your duty to a cause that required you to kill? To a company that would lay you off at the smallest downturn in profits? To parents who mistreated you? Our greatest duty, we were often told, was to ourselves, which meant we had no duty greater than self-interest.

But now duty loomed up as the defining condition of my life, much in the way, I thought, that Parkinson's disease defined my wife's. It felt like a great challenge, an occasion to which I believed I could rise. Unlike my mother, who found satisfaction in serving others, I was not by temperament selfless. Martyrdom, even figurative martyrdom, held little appeal. I did, however, possess a certain stoic streak. And part of me felt I had always been destined to be dealt a bad hand. I was prepared to do my duty.

Maureen, guilty about the damper her medical condition had put on our life, needed more reassurance than ever. She needed to be reassured, specifically, that I wasn't staying with her out of a sense of duty. Furthermore, the disease had made her dependent on me in a way she would have found unimaginable in earlier years, which contributed to the erosion of her confidence. For her to admit this dependence would have undermined her confidence even further. She was appalled by the possibility that I might consider her a burden. As the disease progressed she took to proclaiming her independence ever more insistently. She didn't need me, she would tell me forcibly, she had supported herself since she was twenty. This made me feel that my sacrifice had gone unrewarded. Here I was doing the honorable thing, the noble thing, and she wouldn't even acknowledge it. What at the time I didn't understand, or couldn't accept, was that in order for my sacrifice to achieve its purpose, I had to pretend I wasn't making one.

After Alex left her husband, an imbalance entered into our relationship. She was no longer an unhappy wife, a trapped victim of circumstances understandably and even bravely seeking the fulfillment and passion her marriage didn't provide. Now, after mustering the strength to leave her husband, she had wound up in the dreaded position of the single woman involved with a married man, the woman who, free herself, has to engage in shamefully furtive games in his behalf, who has to wait for that weekday evening or that Sunday afternoon he can steal from his official life, who has to sleep alone while he returns to his family. She hadn't anticipated the loneliness of her new life: the long, empty evenings sitting with a stack of magazines in a black leather chair, eating rice cakes with peanut butter, flicking restlessly between colorized Westerns, CNN updates on the crisis in the Gulf, and sitcoms in which, after every joke, the actors froze like statues while the laugh track played.

She also hadn't realized until then how few true friends she herself had. She and her husband had encountered the world as a couple, and most of their friends were couples. It was not a question of whose side those couples chose in the divorce; couples seek out other couples for equilibrium. Seeing her alone created the sensation of asymmetry, and as time passed they drifted away.

"I spent the weekend at my mother's," she told me one Monday morning, "and when I came back I went to check my phone machine, but the light wasn't blinking. There wasn't a single message. A whole weekend had gone by, and not one person had called me."

She began to pressure me to leave my wife. I had made it clear that, particularly in light of my wife's medical condition, this wasn't going to happen. At first she didn't believe me, then she thought she could change my mind, and for a while after that she tried to console herself with the idea that only circumstances kept us apart.

"Would you leave her if she didn't have a medical condition?" she asked one night.

"I don't know."

"What do you think?"

"It's a hypothetical question."

"But would you? *I have to know.*"

"It's impossible to say."

"You must know. You must. Tell me."

"If she didn't have the problem we might have split up a long time ago. On the other hand, we might have been able to work things out. Or the marriage might not have gotten into trouble in the first place."

"Well, which one is it?"

"I don't know."

Alex became convinced that I was burdening myself with an obsolete sense of duty, that this sense of duty hindered me from seeing things clearly, and that I needed to be shown where happiness lay. To her it was all quite simple: we were in love and nothing should stand in the way of true love.

I didn't tell her this, because it sounded sour and cynical, but the fact was I had become suspicious of "love" as a justification or rationalization for action. It was too convenient and self-serving, and it was disconcertingly opaque. The word "love," I thought, was a lot like the word "evil." Both words described states of mind but not their causes. If, in the therapeutic age in which we live, "evil" is an insufficient explanation of motive, then so is love.

When I was in college I had a young philosophy professor who taught Plato with almost religious passion. He became particularly ecstatic when discussing Platonic ideals such as love. When I told him one day that I wasn't sure I believed in love, he smiled and said, "That's because you've never been in love." I assumed at the time he knew something I didn't know, but I think now that my assumption was incorrect. He was entranced with an ideal, in love with love, so to speak, which is why to explain it he had to resort to poetry:

> ". . . Love is not love
> Which alters when it alteration finds,
> Or bends with the remover to remove.
> O no, it is an ever-fixèd mark . . ."

If it's perfect, it's love, Shakespeare seems to be saying, if it's anything less than perfect, it's something less than love. That now strikes me as a tautology, an empty literary conceit. It's not that I don't "believe" in love; even back in college I was playing the devil's advocate. I am comfortable with the word and, to resort to the language of psychology, the affective state it describes, and I use it freely. I love my daughter, my parents and sisters, Lone Mountain. I love the boy I had been at age five, the slant of the late-afternoon light on Napeague Bay. I understood the owner's love of her dog, the farmer's love of his land, the Catholic's love of the saints. But it is easiest to love, I thought, when we don't expect much in return. When the people or things we love are either completely indifferent to us or utterly dependent on us or bound to us by blood. Romantic love is different. Our own wants and needs hopelessly complicate it. How did we disentangle it from infatuation, sexual desire, status imperatives, the longing for unconditional acceptance? Romantic love could be redemptive and exalting and sacrificial. At its best it may, as I had told the rabbi who married me and Maureen, represent the divine within us. But it could also be greedy and destructive. It could account for astonishing selfishness.

If I had any doubts about that, they were swept away by a phone call around that time from my father. He said he had run into his old friend Scott Hopkinson, whom he hadn't seen in several years, and Scott told him that his wife, Lisa, had left him. Lisa and Scott had been married for more than three decades. My family had known them for much of that time. Scott Hopkinson, who came from a prosperous Baltimore family, was a gifted man; some of his colleagues, including my father, considered him a genius. He had mastered several languages, including Russian and Farsi, and his administrative skills and political instincts had enabled him to rise to the top of his profession. Effortlessly articulate, a natural raconteur and irresistible wit, he tended to dominate a roomful of people.

Lisa was quiet, not because her husband intimidated or overshadowed her. She had composure and intelligence; her quiet was the quiet of contemplation, the quiet of someone listening to an inner voice. She had delicate features—a narrow high-bridged nose, bright pale eyes, flaxen hair she usually kept in a bun—but she never appeared weak or overrefined. In fact, and this was the most extraordinary thing about her, she had a kind of subsurface sexual radiance, a glow or aura that was altogether distinct from her beauty. Even the most indifferent men felt it. She was my mother's age, but when we were in the same room together I found it hard to take my eyes off her.

Scott's career had involved postings in the Middle East and Asia but the family—they had three children: a smart girl, a pretty girl, and a wild but charming boy—had always returned to the large and comfortable old house Scott had inherited on the Eastern Shore. When the children were grown and the eldest daughter had children of her own, Lisa began to accompany Scott less often on his trips. The month in Riyadh, the six-week swing through the Pacific Rim, the summer in St. Petersburg—they were tiring. She preferred spending time with her grandchildren.

Two summers ago, Scott was in Ankara organizing an international conference on maritime law when Lisa called him. Robert Carson, she said, had asked her to marry him. Scott was speechless. Lisa was fifty-three at the time and had never, to her husband, to my parents, or to any of her friends, given any outward sign of dissatisfaction with her marriage. But what made the news so profoundly stunning to Scott—and what to me made it echo with mystery and longing when my father told me about it— was that Robert Carson was Scott's oldest, closest friend. They had been roommates in prep school. Robert had been the best man at Scott and Lisa's wedding. Robert was also the heir to an immense fortune, a billionaire, according to *Forbes*.

Lisa went on, during that phone conversation, to say she was calling from the airport. Robert, who was waiting for her in his private jet, had told her he had been in love with her his entire life. Her children were grown, he had said. They were both now in their mid-fifties. The time had come to act. Robert was prepared to divorce Anne, his third wife, if Lisa would leave Scott. Over the phone, Lisa told her husband, standing speechless in a crowded conference room in an Ankara hotel, that she had decided to accept Robert's proposal. She was leaving with him for Paris in a few minutes.

Scott, shocked to the core of his being, returned to Washington and took a leave of absence from his job. He felt confused and defeated. Weeks passed, and then months. He had always had an enormous appetite for work but now he could find nothing to do that interested him. Instead of returning to work, he took early retirement. His children felt as betrayed as he did. At first they refused to see or speak to their mother, but as time passed they softened and she began to visit them. However, they refused to allow Robert, whom they had grown up regarding as an uncle, to accompany her. Robert divorced Anne and gave her the house in Oyster Bay. He and Lisa traveled, staying for weeks on end in penthouse suites in the most expensive hotels in Biarritz, Florence, Tokyo. Anne contacted Scott and the two of them spent much time discussing what had happened. Scott replayed his entire marriage again and again, searching for the clues that he, the brilliant student of human affairs, had missed, unable to forgive himself for having failed so egregiously to understand the two people who had been closest to him.

We, his friends, were just as mystified. Had Lisa and Robert been having an affair all these years? we wondered. Both of them had sworn to their families that they hadn't, but that meant nothing. Was this an exhilarating example of true love, of two people who were meant to be together finally finding each other after thirty years? That was how Lisa portrayed it to her children. Robert was, like Lisa, quiet. With his money he had never had to work, and had led a somewhat aimless life, dabbling in philanthropy. Scott had always secretly considered Robert a weak man and believed Robert had envied him his independence, his success, his force of personality. Was stealing Lisa an act of revenge? Or was

Robert a man who simply wanted what he couldn't have and felt that because of his vast fortune he was entitled to it? Was Lisa a woman who, despite the fact that Scott's family was not without money, had been unable to resist the lure of that fortune? Or had we all been wrong and had Lisa in fact felt overshadowed all those years by her brilliant husband? Had she longed for the companionship of someone less gifted, someone who was not always the center of attention? What went on in her heart at night, we wondered, as she lay next to the sleeping billionaire she had married? Was the contentment she felt with him adequate compensation for the anguish she knew she had caused Scott and her children? We would never know, and that made all of us, their friends, less certain about ourselves, for it reminded us that we never really knew anyone else.

A year after the divorce, Lisa and Robert passed through Washington on their jet, and from the airport Lisa called her daughter, who lived in Fairfax. Her daughter invited Lisa out to the house. Lisa said Robert was with her and asked if he could come along. The daughter refused.

"He wants to be your friend," Lisa told her daughter.

"He was my father's friend," the daughter replied.

Afterward, whenever I heard someone talking about "true love," I thought of that line—*He was my father's friend*—and I wondered if it was through such betrayals that love proved itself true.

Chapter 19

I had told a couple of close friends about the affair, and Alex had done the same—even confiding, I was a little disconcerted to learn, in her mother. From time to time Alex and I would go out to dinner with these friends—and their husbands or wives or dates (never with Alex's mother; the one time Alex mentioned she wanted her to meet me I pretended I hadn't heard)—and the point of the evening would be for everyone to act as if Alex and I were just another couple. While these charades made me feel uncomfortable, they stirred Alex's desire to legitimize our relationship. She began to urge friends of mine to convince me I ought to leave my wife. One of the people she partially succeeded in enlisting in this project was Josh Hammer. While he did not campaign on her behalf, he had become sympathetic to her dilemma, and he decided I was taking advantage of her.

"If you're not going to marry her, you should end the relationship," Josh told me one September afternoon. We were sitting on Parisian metal chairs beside a combed-gravel path in the trim, groomed park adjacent to the public library. The sun was descending toward the western rim of the skyscrapers enclosing the park; their shadows edged toward us.

I had known Josh for years. He was a foreign correspondent and had flown into town the week before, after covering a coup in Liberia. It was the kind of life I had once wanted to live; he felt isolated and ignored in Africa, however, and wanted the life I had.

"Why?" I asked. "We're both grown-ups."

His disapproval, since I had seen him treat women heartlessly, surprised me. Alex must have argued her case with conviction, but then, she was in sales, a professional persuader.

"She knew what she was getting into," I went on. "In fact, she went after me. She took the initiative. She was the aggressor. *She* seduced me."

I disliked the way I sounded, whining and finger-pointing like the five-year-olds in my daughter's kindergarten, but the idea that I should somehow be held responsible for entrapping Alex, and now keeping her imprisoned, simply did not, I felt, square with the facts.

"After we became involved, I never misled her," I said. "I never promised her I'd leave my wife. In fact, I've done just the opposite. I've made it very clear that I *won't* leave. So the decision isn't mine. The decision is Alex's."

"But she's not going to leave you. She loves you. And she can't help hoping that one day you'll realize how much happier you'd be with her."

"I don't know if I would. I don't think I would. I've told her that. I've said that if I left my wife for her, any improvement in my life would be canceled out by the guilt I would feel for abandoning my family."

"She thinks you just need convincing. She's told me *I* have to make you realize how much happier you'd be with her. She thinks I have an obligation as your friend to do that."

"You don't. And I wouldn't."

"As long as you continue to see her she's going to tell herself there's a possibility of changing your mind. She'll continue to work at it. If you care for her at all, if you respect her, you should end the relationship so she can be free to go find someone who will give her what she wants."

"Why should I do that? Like I said, she's a grown-up. I'm not misleading her. If she wants to end the relationship and move on, she can do that. I'd never pressure her into continuing to see me."

"That proves you don't really care about her. You're using her. If you cared about her, you'd leave her. For her own good."

"These moral distinctions are too fine for me."

"You're being selfish."

"No. But I'm not a martyr, either."

The acknowledgment made me feel savage. I was operating outside the Judeo-Christian ethical framework, in a Darwinian system in which strength was virtue and weakness fatal. The strong were pitiless, and took from the weak without remorse. It was a clarifying but not particularly comforting idea. As our conversation drew to a close, the sun slipped behind the tall buildings surrounding the park. The combed paths, with silver and russet late-summer flowers massed in their margins, were engulfed in shadow. With the shadows came a chill. Fall lay just ahead, and then winter, which promised to be cold.

As the days grew shorter, Alex turned resentful. The approach of the end of the year underscored her sense that time was running out for her. Her second-class status, her illicit, illegitimate role in my life, galled her. She became aggressive and demanding. Periods of low-grade hostility were punctuated by angry outbursts. Just as she had begun to provoke her husband when her marriage began to feel confining, she now began provoking me. She called me at home and refused to end the conversation.

"Maureen's here, I've got to go," I said.

"I don't care. I'm not going to get off the phone just because Maureen's there."

"I've got to go."

"Don't hang up on me. *Don't.*"

I hung up.

Alex had begun the affair out of anger at her husband, to punish him. It had been a way of precipitating a crisis in her life, of forcing it in a new direction. She had succeeded, but the outcome wasn't what she had hoped it would be. Now she had become as angry at me as she had been at her husband, and she was trying to precipitate a crisis in the affair. The next time we talked she told me she didn't want to hear from me again unless I was going to leave my wife. I thought that this was a good idea and stopped calling her.

The following week she called up a woman I worked with and invited her out to lunch. The woman assumed the lunch had a business purpose. In the middle of the meal, Alex burst into tears. She told the woman she had told me not to call her unless I was going to leave my wife and so I hadn't. Now she wanted the woman to persuade me to call her. The woman felt awkward. The people at the next table, in the midst of a genuine business lunch, kept glancing over, furtively curious. The woman told Alex she was sorry but didn't see that there was anything she could do.

Three weeks later I was working in my office when the phone rang. It was Alex.

"Why haven't you called?" she asked. Her tone was aggrieved, belligerent.

"You told me you didn't want me to call," I said.

"Don't you miss me?"

"Sure." The truth was I didn't miss her. I was tired of the agonizing, tired of the resentment, the sulks, the accusations.

"Then why didn't you call?"

"Alex . . ."

I'd had an affair to escape the burden of marriage, and the affair had become as burdensome as the marriage. By mid-December, when a foot of snow from an unanticipated blizzard brought the city to a halt, it was over.

Chapter 20

I settled in to experience the grim satisfactions of duty. It made me see myself at a distance. I was not living my life—generating a personal history through an ongoing encounter with the world—so much as performing a series of ritual motions. This sensation, of repeatedly enacting a repertoire of circumscribed gestures, had its advantages. It gave the days a certain mechanical regularity. My wife, my daughter, and I rose at seven-thirty, and Jessica and I left the house just before nine. She was by then in kindergarten, with bangs and long blond hair my wife usually pulled back in a ponytail. Her best friend was Melissa. Jessica had developed the ability to draw with a line so confident and simple it reminded me of Matisse, and she lived content in the assumption of the five-year-old that her parents could and would always protect her from harm. It was to her altogether natural that we hold hands on our morning walk.

After dropping her at her school and nodding to the mothers in sweatsuits, who seemed increasingly surly and oppressed, I fought my way onto the subway, spent the day in a congenial office, returned home in time for a stiff drink, and, after dinner, cleaned the dishes and read to my daughter before winding up in bed with a book. Outwardly our life seemed normal.

But days could pass in which my wife and I didn't talk except to discuss household logistics. We lived without a shared sense of the future. We never planned ahead. Consequently we missed the transition into middle-class homeownership that virtually every other couple we knew had made—that move out of the rental apartment and into that small first co-op, or the brownstone in the marginal area, or the "starter" Colonial in a less distinctive suburb that begins the upward progression into the real estate heaven of American life. We remained renters.

Nonetheless, I told myself, I had made a commitment to my marriage—to the idea of it anyway. As the social reactionaries wanted, I was prepared to sacrifice my own happiness to fulfill my responsibilities. That was the noblest reason. There were others. "We thought you liked being miserable," one of my sisters once told me. And it was true. The freedom to luxuriate in self-pity is one of the consolations of a marriage gone wrong. Failure can be gratifying, even liberating; it relieves you of the need to aspire. Also, in some primordial layer of my brain, I was superstitious, afraid that, if I abdicated my responsibilities, I would bring even greater misfortune on myself. After all, if you make your own luck, you also make your own misfortune.

The dutiful life is a reduced one, and without intending to, my wife and I stripped away the extraneous. We were seeing fewer of the people we'd met when we first moved to the neighborhood. They sensed the troubles in our marriage and it spooked them. And we lacked the brute energy, the calories, to keep a social life burning. We learned to survive, like animals in a drought, by keeping still and doing very little. I had the sense that I was biding my time, waiting for the rains.

———————

It was during this period, seven years into my marriage, that I realized I was losing my temper more easily and more often. I am not a volatile person—people who meet me for the first time have been known to describe me as aloof, a characterization that saddens me because, although it may be accurate in a limited way, it's not how I think of myself—but I do have a temper. The aloofness made for a very thin veneer. And it was growing thinner. My ability to tolerate annoyances had diminished radically. Any small disturbance could provoke a flooding sense of panic. Minor frustrations—the stuck storm window, snarled traffic—enraged me so often that Jessica learned to anticipate my reactions and would warn, in the tone of an adult admonishing an unruly child, "Patience, Dad."

The car alarm had been developed by then, but not yet the timer that automatically switched it off, and these in particular—the bloodcurdling shriek emitted hour after hour from an inert and insensate vehicle parked just up the block—could bring me to tears of desperation. It amazed me that other people could remain oblivious to the sound, but they could. I would see it happen. "How can you stand the noise?" I cried, frantically, to one of my neighbors, a bearded assistant district attorney contentedly walking his Lhasa apso past a blaring Toyota Camry, wired so its lights flashed in time with the siren. "I don't hear it," he said.

Like the rabbits who live around airport runways, the attorney had evolved a mental circuitry that enabled him to switch off the noise. I couldn't do this; it was like living a lie. The contradiction between the beautiful block, with its twin rows of low-lying brownstones, its wrought-iron fences, its cherry and willow and sycamore trees and the deafening howl of an alarm we had no choice but to endure created a cognitive dissonance so piercing I was afraid it would drive me insane. One night the following spring, the unstoppable braying of a car alarm on the street outside finally pushed me over the edge. I threw off the sheets, pulled on a pair of pants, and, in the dark, rummaged through the closet for the baseball bat. "What are you doing?" my wife asked. I ignored her and rushed down to the street. The alarm was coming from a faded maroon Volvo with an I ♥ WELLFLEET bumper sticker. I swung the bat against a window, expecting it to shatter, but the glass proved surprisingly sturdy. I swung again. A web of cracks appeared. On the third swing the window exploded inward. I turned to the hood, crumpling the metal with repeated blows, punishing this car first for disturbing my peace, then for all the shrieking alarms I had ever heard, and then for all the trials I was forced to endure. Finally, the siren stopped. I had killed it. The thought filled me with satisfaction. When I returned to the bedroom my wife looked at me with an expression of horror. "You're crazy," she said. I could tell she was thinking, *If he'll do that to a car he might do it to me.*

I was aware at the time of the stupidity and danger of this behavior. People were murdered during such inane confrontations. There had been a story in the papers about a man who was shot in Little Italy when a dispute about a parking space got out of hand. An idiotic death arising out of a pointless argument.

Nonetheless, I couldn't control myself. One night, I assaulted a cabdriver on Forty-second Street when he refused to take me to Brooklyn. I remember another time during this period, when I was driving Jessica through one of the borough's old neighborhoods on the way to see her pediatrician. It was a Saturday morning. The narrow streets were clogged with double-parked cars and the policemen ticketing them, bag-laden shoppers who ignored the DON'T WALK signs, and hot dog vendors swatting the greasy smoke that poured from their carts. The man in the car behind us began honking the instant the light at an intersection turned green. He honked when I yielded to pedestrians. He honked when I slowed at an unoccupied section of curb that I hoped was a parking spot but that turned out to harbor a fire hydrant. That third time he honked, I pulled the car over and got out. He stopped to swear at me for driving so slowly. I can remember his leaning his stonelike head out the window of his old Buick and working his big jaw as he screamed denunciation. Without thinking, I charged toward his car and landed a flying kick against the door. He accelerated away, tires squealing, stopped after twenty feet, and shouted back, "You're crazy, you know that! You're fuckin' crazy!"

I turned back to my daughter. She was watching me through the windshield with large eyes and a still face. *"You're crazy!"* That was what my wife had said as well, and I realized that I *was* crazy, that I had become one of the city's foaming, snarling, murderous maniacs.

Chapter 21

I didn't think of it in these terms at the time, and my behavior certainly didn't suggest it, but what I was searching for in those days was moral clarification. The fatalism I had felt in childhood had given way, in my twenties, to a cult of ambition, which had yielded in my thirties to the formalistic stoicism of what I had taken to thinking of as the masks of life. But these ethical systems, steeped in superstition and misconceived grandiosity, were like primitive forms of idolatry. Fatalism and ambition had long since ceased to sustain me, and I was unable, in the end, to adapt to the masks of life. They were rigid, stultifying. Although not scrupulously honest, I had nonetheless been acculturated with the ideals of honesty to an extent I had not appreciated. I was a prisoner of moral conventions I thought I disdained.

In the midst of this confusion, I flew out to Los Angeles on business. It was a routine assignment, the kind of thing that had excited me years ago but now no longer did. In between appointments I sat on the couch in my hotel room and dictated my thoughts into a tape recorder. I conceived of this as an exercise in self-analysis. I had been ambivalent before—my life could be seen

as a series of studies in ambivalence—but never had I felt so overwhelmed by chaos. Conflicting impulses surged through me like
crosscurrents in an estuary. If I could just put my feelings into
words, I thought, I could achieve some clarity.

It took a few tries to overcome the procedural awkwardness—the throat clearing, the check of the tiny ruby-red battery
light, the fumbling for the pause button when my mind stalled in
midthought—but I persisted, and after a few sessions filled two
sides of a ninety-minute tape with ramblings on the tension between fulfillment and duty. The experience of talking aloud didn't
bring me any insight. I started to play the tape back but couldn't
stand the sound of my own voice, the hesitant narcissistic groping,
the anguish and self-pity, and I turned it off and threw it away.

I hated the idea that I might be one of those people who are never
at home in the world, who resist their life whatever direction it takes
and who die without ever feeling they truly belonged where they
were. So when someone posted a notice for a sublet on the bulletin
board at my office, I decided to take it. The time had come to go.

I took Maureen out to a Mexican restaurant to explain the
situation. The restaurant was dark and crowded. Longhorn skulls,
spotlit with recessed lighting, adorned the walls. Music, a tele-
vised basketball game, and the jabbering, smoking crowd at the
bar all competed to be heard.

I told Maureen I'd decided to move out. We weren't getting
along, I said. It would be a "trial separation."

"Why now?" Maureen asked.

I hadn't prepared an answer and my response was unsatisfy-
ing, almost incoherent. I'd had an affair, I said. The affair was over,
but the whole experience had made it senseless for us to carry on.

Maureen started to cry. "Why are you telling me this?" she
asked. "Why? Why?"

I hadn't realized that it was too late for honesty. Honesty, if applied selectively, at one's convenience, is dishonest. The opportunistic confession is self-serving. It buys a very cheap form of peace. I felt as if I had thrust a knife right into my wife's heart.

Despite my confession, Maureen didn't want me to leave. She said the next day that for Jessica's sake we should stay together, see a marriage counselor, and try to work things out. I refused. I had made up my mind, I said. I was going.

Maureen worried about Jessica. How would we explain it to our daughter? she wondered. I said we didn't need to tell her. I often worked late. I was often away on business. We could finesse the entire matter for the time being. She was only five years old. She wouldn't even notice.

One early summer morning a few days later, while Maureen was out and Jessica was at school, I packed some clothes, a few books, a table, and a futon I'd bought into my small Ford Tempo and moved to my new home. I felt like a criminal fleeing the scene of a crime, a guilty convict escaping prison. I didn't deserve to be free, I thought, but I was.

The apartment I had sublet occupied the back half of the parlor floor of a brownstone three miles away. There was only one room, but it had a high ceiling and a small fireplace. There was also a bathroom and kitchen, and floor-to-ceiling windows with rotting mullions that looked out onto a garden with an old dogwood tree and a moss-stained brick wall. It took very little time for me to set the place up. I deciphered the seemingly illogical system by which the back and the seat of the futon frame swung apart on one set of wooden hinges and then locked into each other on a second set to form a platform, bolted them together, and heaved the futon, covered in rough white canvas, onto the frame. I attached the lathe-rounded legs to the wobbly table I'd bought to use as a desk when I moved to the city ten years earlier and placed it against the windows. I set out on its unvarnished surface a cheap brass lamp and my pencil container, a felt-covered tin can my youngest sister had made for me as a Christmas gift when she was nine. I stacked my books against the wall. The two glasses and two plates I had brought with me took up one half of one shelf in the kitchen's cupboard. The only closet was in the bathroom. I laid out my socks, underwear, towels, and shirts on its three lined shelves. And then I sat down on the futon.

I was utterly alone and had absolutely nothing to do. Reading was impossible, it was too early for a drink, and even if I had a drink, what would I do once I had finished it? The room was so small I couldn't really move around. I considered taking a walk, but that would have made me feel I was fleeing the place. I sat there, and as twilight came on and the light faded from the tall windows, I realized I had made a terrible mistake.

When I awoke the following morning, the sensation of dismay immediately surged back over me. It was to remain in the weeks ahead. Still, I had left Maureen in order to be free to do what I wanted to do and I resolved to get out on the town. I accepted invitations from people I hardly knew. I stood in the noisy living rooms of decorators I had flatteringly profiled, making conversation with splenetic industrialists and their gaunt wives, people as uninterested in me as I was in them. I spent time in nightclubs with an aging rogue who, at fifty, had run through three wives and an inheritance of several million dollars and who, while his date was in the bathroom, would try to pick up the waitress when she appeared with our drinks. I put in appearances at downtown literary salons presided over by the professionally vivacious. I was making the scene, I told myself, this was fun, this was why I had left Maureen. But at some point in the evening the crushing pointlessness of it all would overtake me. What am I *doing* here? I would wonder—this is not who I am. And I would slink out and take the long ride in the groaning, usually empty subway back to the small apartment.

The man who worked in the front half of the parlor floor I was subletting lived in the apartment overhead. He was on his second marriage, to a woman twelve years younger than he was. They had a small son whose shrieks of laughter and thumping footsteps coming through the plaster ceiling reminded me of the family life I was missing, the daughter I now only saw sporadically. The man supported himself by writing service articles for travel magazines, compiling exhaustive lists of New England inns and Caribbean resorts, with their prices, the details of accommodation, and terse notes on local attractions. He didn't make much money doing this, but he seemed to enjoy it. He was in his late forties and struck me as a contented man. He knew about my "trial separation," and one afternoon, when he had just closed an article on Bucks County bed-and-breakfasts, we fell into a discussion of the vagaries of marriage.

"I saw my first wife the other day," he said. "She's a perfectly nice woman. I don't know why I left her. It was clear to me then. I thought it was a matter of survival. But I don't understand it at all now. It was the times, I think, the sixties. It had nothing to do with her and everything to do with the times."

The nonchalance of this confession was startling. Are we all opaque to ourselves, I wondered, buffeted by impulses we can only understand, if at all, years later? Was I? The possibility chilled me. And then there was my neighbor's talk about "the times." It occurred to me that I might be just as much a prisoner, or victim, of my times as he had been of his. My times, the onset of the last decade of the twentieth century, were vastly different from the sixties, but they were, I had no doubt, just as rigidly encased in their own invisible pathologies.

Maureen had thought that even if I moved out we should see a marriage counselor. If we didn't solve our problems, she had said, we could at least figure out what went wrong and why. It would help us, for Jessica's sake, to remain friends down the road. This undertaking did not appeal to me. I was already living with the fear that I had been wrong to leave. An investigation of our marriage, under a therapist's oversight, might establish that it *was* in fact a mistake, and then what would I do? Still, for my daughter's sake, I swallowed my misgivings and consented.

Maureen found a therapist who worked in the neighborhood. On our very first visit, arriving early, we ran into the parents of one of Jessica's schoolmates as they were leaving—the husband had a perennially defeated air; the wife, a shrewd prying woman, was a fixture among the gossiping mothers clustered on the sidewalk in front of the school every morning—and exchanged sheepish nods. It was a moment of acute, almost thrilling embarrassment; we both now knew the other's deepest secret, and the knowledge that the other couple also had hidden troubles offset the shame of exposure. We were not alone.

I wondered how many of the other parents, the ones we'd see on Parents' Day circulating politely through the noisy classrooms, had similar secrets. I suspected many of them did. Why? Were we weaker people than our parents? Did we have less self-control, a diminished sense of duty? Did we suffer from defective character? I did not believe so. We lived in an age in which commitment had been bled out of the culture and which was, instead, saturated with temptation. When our parents came of age, commitment, or at least the appearance of commitment, had been rewarded, and at times enforced. We lived in an altogether different environment. Surrounded by disposable goods, we were urged every day to switch brands, trade up, discard, satisfy every appetite, gratify desires artificially induced by advertising. Our times encouraged faithlessness. We couldn't count on our society to instill or even promote commitment. If we wanted it, we would have to kindle it ourselves in our individual souls.

This became clear in those initial therapy sessions. The therapist was a matronly woman who seemed composed of cubes: broad shoulders; a square chin; an oblong helmet of dark hair. She used her thick fingers to frame earnest questions. She had a plodding, methodical way, after one of us had made some point, of turning to the other and saying, "Well, Maureen, what do you think?" or "Well, John, how do you respond to that?" I felt sorry for the woman, pitied her for the futility of her task. How could she possibly reconcile conflicting versions of reality? It was like trying to build a tower in the dark, fumbling blindly for bricks that may or may not even be there. After half a dozen sessions, we stopped going.

Chapter 22

Sometime after Independence Day of that year, I started seeing Jill
Hartmann. She was a small woman who didn't think of herself
as small, with a mass of wiry hair and brilliant blue eyes, eyes that
flashed and glittered and shone.

The first time we went out for dinner, at a small restaurant
with a stamped-tin ceiling and a carved mahogany bar, she reached
across the table and took my hand.

"Why are you still wearing this?" she asked, fingering my
wedding ring. It was a plain gold band. Maureen and I had picked
out our rings in a shop in Boston, where we were living at the
time, and had had the date of our marriage, 12/19/82, engraved
on the inside surface.

"I don't know." It had never occurred to me to remove the
ring. I had worn it for seven years. I was used to its weight, and
whenever I took it off its absence nagged at me.

"I thought you had left your wife," Jill said.

"I have."

"So why are you wearing it?"

"Habit, I guess." I didn't see that it was anyone's concern but
mine.

She looked at me with her brimming porcelain eyes. "But you've left your wife," she persisted.

It was only then that I realized how momentous the issue was for her. Like most single women, she had vowed to herself, she explained later, that she would never become involved with a married man. Women who did, she felt, were abject. They were destined for defeat. It humiliated her to be seen in a restaurant with a man wearing a wedding ring. It marked her, in her mind, as publicly as a brand.

"You're right," I said.

I started to slip the ring off my finger. But I felt a deep pull of resistance. It wasn't just that I'd grown accustomed to the ring and felt incomplete without it. I was also still attached to my marriage. I was reluctant to declare it finished, and I didn't like the idea that someone was demanding that I do so. But I overcame my resistance, removed the ring, and slipped it into my pocket. Beneath my knuckle, where I had worn the ring, a ghostly band of paleness encircled my finger, which now felt denuded and exposed.

"Thank you," Jill said.

Jill had the capacity to invest the most ordinary objects and quotidian moments with a tremulous, radiant significance. It was part of her passionate nature. She was so passionate, in fact, so beset by the turbulence of desire, love, and empathy, that sometimes she appeared slightly unstable. She was an artist, from coastal Oregon. Her father had made a small fortune investing in medical technology, part of the venture capital group that funded the development of magnetic resonance imaging, and he supported her, not luxuriously, but with just enough money so she never had to work. Free from economic exigencies, she was able to see her life entirely in terms of possibilities. She could devote herself to her painting without ever having to show or sell or even complete any particular canvas.

Although she didn't have a job, she maintained a frantic schedule. She awoke at six to teach a yoga class at seven—for the exercise, not the money—then spent the day at her studio, where she painted and held meetings with aspiring architects and film directors and choreographers on various projects she and they were entertaining. In the evenings she went to openings, screenings, poetry readings, book parties. There was always something. Her Filofax was crammed with appointments; its scratched oxblood leather cover had become as soft as cloth from constant use. She was the first person I knew to own a cellular phone, which she used while walking through Washington Square with her gym bag slung over her shoulder, or while painting, or while making a spaghetti sauce for an impromptu dinner party, to check in with her vast array of friends and update and revise her schedule.

She traveled constantly. She was always flying back to Portland to see her ailing father or off to London to attend a wedding. And she moved constantly. When I first met her she was living in a sprawling shabby apartment she shared with an older woman. It was lit with candles and infested with mice. But they had a disagreement soon after she and I started seeing each other—Jill refused to specify what it concerned—and she found temporary lodgings in a tiny apartment above a garment-district noodle shop. It was owned by a Buddhist monk, and when he returned from a retreat at a Catskills monastery, she moved into a brick-walled loft in an industrial neighborhood. A photographer owned the loft; she rented a windowless room in the rear.

The studio in which she worked was also windowless. It was on the fourth floor of a rotting cast-iron building; the threshing of the machinery in the Chinese garment factory overhead caused the walls to quiver. The gay costume designer who held the lease on the floor had set up his shop in the rear, with its mammoth windows, and subdivided the rest into large gloomy cubicles, which he sublet to artists like Jill. The air was thick with the odors of linseed oil and turpentine. The floorboards were spongy. Some grinding form of punk rock was usually playing on a paint-splattered cassette recorder.

Jill threw herself heedlessly into one project after another, putting each aside, incomplete, when she was overtaken by a new enthusiasm. She stopped work on a meditation pyramid for the homeless to start an autobiographical novel, logging fourteen-hour days on the laptop computer her father bought her, but then she abandoned the book to research a documentary film about a Tamil dance troupe. Her paintings—sketchy brushwork and tentative blots of color on otherwise bare canvases—seemed unfinished too. It took me a while to grasp that she had no real interest in conventional accomplishment. What she loved was to lose herself in the ecstasies of creation.

Jill treated our relationship like one of her new projects. She saw it as another avenue for self-discovery, a fresh opportunity for creative exploration. I became, that summer, the repository of all her vibrating expectations. We spent hours drinking red wine and talking about ourselves: about our pasts, our families, our temperaments and predilections. I marveled at first at the inexhaustibility of our conversations, at the brimming vividness of the times we spent together. Once, when she was sleeping at my place, a thunderstorm awoke me in the middle of the night, and when I sat up I saw her crouched naked at the open window. Rain spattered on the wooden floor. Outside, the undersides of the dogwood leaves fluttered whitely in the incandescent lightning bursts. She sat on her heels, pale and motionless, transfixed by the storm. I was going to ask her what she was thinking but thought better of it and lay back, listening to the rain and wind rattle the leaves and watching, whenever a bolt of lightning irradiated the room, their agitated shadows dance along the wall.

Jill expected me to support her artistic enterprises, and I did my best, but after a while the futility of the project-hopping began to wear me down. I told her she needed to identify what she did best and devote herself to that. It was difficult enough, I said, to succeed in one field. She felt that I didn't understand why she did what she did. She wasn't deeply interested in success, she said, she had an irrepressible need to express herself. While on one level I admired her attitude, which suggested a priestly purity of motive, I considered myself a professional and I began to find these various artistic forays dismayingly amateurish and undisciplined. They seemed, in the self-absorption they entailed, bereft and stunted. I began to look at our relationship in the same light. It was a series of vivid moments devoid of sequence, leading nowhere, a cluster of fragments that, like one of Jill's paintings, failed to cohere into a picture.

One day toward the end of the summer I put my ring back on. My hand had felt imbalanced without it. And I hadn't left my wife in order to have another woman tell me what I could and could not do. I was startled to find that the next time I saw Jill she noticed *immediately*.

"You're wearing your ring," she said.

"Yes. But I'm not making a statement. I missed it. I was used to it. I played with it."

"But you've left your wife."

"That's right. And frankly I didn't leave her just to have you tell me what to do. I can't stand to be told what to do."

"But if you've left her—"

"*Nobody* tells me what to do."

Her porcelain eyes welled. A few days later, when I met her closest friend at the opening of the friend's exhibit (muddy smeared paintings displayed in a Chelsea bank lobby, amid blocky signs advertising interest rates on home loans and CD's), the friend snubbed me as a married man caddishly taking advantage of

Jill, a conclusion that seemed to me horribly unjust but that nonetheless contained a logic I had to acknowledge.

Jill couldn't tolerate the fact that I had put my ring back on. We had tempestuous debates lasting through the night. She would sob and remonstrate. She had an almost Jesuitical ability to worry a question for hours. I couldn't tolerate the demands she was making on me—I couldn't tolerate the *idea* that she was making demands—and would counterattack angrily. The more we argued, the wearier I became. I missed my wife and daughter. I missed our home. I didn't belong where I was. I belonged instead back with them. What did it matter if I wasn't, in some narrow sense, happy? I wasn't happy living on my own either, or in the society of aging rakes, fey costume designers, and aspiring painters. Maybe, I thought, happiness just wasn't in the cards for me.

Anyway, I had never quite understood what happiness was, had never acquired a firm grip on the concept. I suspected that the people who pursued it the most avidly hadn't either. Elation, glee, contentment, triumph, satisfaction, relief—I understood all those, but happiness? It was too broad, too vague, too overarching and all-encompassing. And it was also, compared with the sense of belonging, shallow. Belonging rooted you, defined you; it pulled at the very core of your being.

Four months after I had moved out, and a few weeks after Jill and I parted for the last time, at night, on a cinematically rain-soaked cobblestoned street beneath the Brooklyn Bridge, I went home.

three

Chapter 23

To get home from work in those days I could take one of two subways: the slow, lumbering F train, which stopped two blocks from our house, or the sleek, swift IRT, with its new graffiti-resistant Japanese cars, which stopped twenty blocks away. I preferred the IRT. The ride itself passed quickly and the arrival at the Grand Army Plaza stop, forty feet below the breathtaking Civil War memorial, was a moment of blissful release, particularly in winter. The crowds, clammy and perspiring after standing in their overcoats in the overheated and tightly packed subway, surged up the stairs from the platform, through the sprocket-grinding exit turnstiles, and up the second flight of stairs into a night in which the frigid and richly oxygenated air was, after spending forty minutes underground, exhilarating.

I also enjoyed the mile-long walk home. I remember coming home one night the winter after I had moved out and then returned. It had snowed, and the snow had first melted and then, when the temperature plummeted, frozen. The branches on the sycamore and gingko trees rimming the Plaza looked as if they had been dipped in glass. The passengers who emerged from the subway with me moved in careful silence along the irregularly shoveled sidewalks—sidestepping ice patches, planting a shoe firmly on scattered salt granules—and then, at the corner near a sumptuous Italian Renaissance dining club built in the nineteenth century and now desperately short of members, dispersed, flooding out across the big avenue and down the side streets.

I headed south, past brownstone and limestone mansions built, along with the sadly obsolete dining club, at a time when the neighborhood was the home for soda-cracker tycoons and mail-order-catalog publishers. The houses were as grand as frigates. Tall stately oaks shadowed their stoops. The flames of the gas lamps planted inside the low stoop walls flickered. The striped canvas awnings above some of the doors were bowed with the frozen snow. I knew, from years of walking this route, all of these houses, and as I passed I looked up into the windows. There was the firelit library with the matched Chinese vases; the narrow parlor with the wedding-cake ceiling molding and the shimmering glass chandelier; the book-lined living room where the amateur string quartet sometimes sat practicing with a concentration so intense it was comical.

The original design of those houses (a garden level for the dining room and kitchen; a main floor of adjoining parlors; a third floor for the bedrooms of husband and wife, each linked but also separated by a central closet; a fourth floor of rooms for the children; and a fifth floor, squeezed beneath the cornice, of cramped cells with eyebrow windows for the servants) and the way they had been altered in the years that followed (converted into duplexes; divided into shabby studios with linoleum-floored kitchenettes built into former closets; and reconverted into single-family residences) reminded me of the extent to which the family is a work in progress. Like those Victorian homes it has undergone continual evolution to accommodate the needs of each new generation.

It started to snow again, a powdery snow that drifted like dust along the sidewalks. Most of the subway passengers had headed off in other directions and I was more or less alone. The tires of a stuck car spun and whined. The driver, a dark blur behind the foggy windshield, cursed and hit the steering wheel. His exasperation, so familiar to me, induced an involuntary spasm of glee; other people's troubles, even as we empathize with them, can make us feel lucky and safe.

I passed the yellowing limestone synagogue and the Greek Orthodox church built of rough, dark fieldstone. The snow drifted like mist from the black sky into the conical orange ambit of the streetlights and was blown by the wind in shifting watery veins along the avenue. I turned down a handsome block embowered by massive oaks. A coating of ice glazed the wrought-iron gates. The street was quiet, the windows of the houses glowed with the promise of shelter. In one, a small boy standing on a chair next to a stove gravely watched his mother frying something in an iron skillet. In another, two houses down, a tired-looking woman faced away from a man, shaking her head while he talked angrily. In a third, a young girl, holding out her white nightgown, jumped off the arm of a couch. In a fourth, two men were waltzing together.

Life in the Victorian period, the life for which those brownstones were designed and which, in its rigid compartmentalization, was so radically different from the lives they now served, had begun to be held up as an idealized model for those nostalgic for the days when the family was a respected institution. Margaret Thatcher, Newt Gingrich, and the conservative historian Gertrude Himmelfarb had all taken to invoking Victorian society as the moral paragon to which we should aspire. *The New Victorians,* a book that came out during those years, examined the emergence of a fashionable sexual prudishness, and a new magazine, *Victoria,* celebrated a kitschified version of nineteenth-century domesticity.

A friend had given my wife and me a small painting from that period. It was done in our neighborhood during the height of the late-Victorian sensibility and depicted a bearded man, dressed in a black suit and seated in a wing chair, reading by an open window.

The park's leafy trees could be seen outside. His wife, her hair in a bun and a bustle in her floor-length dress, poured tea while two children played ball on a carpet near the man's feet. The tranquillity of the scene, the harmony it conveyed, depended of course on the husband's centrality and authority and the wife's complete submission to it.

That winter I was reading Fraser Harrison's *Dark Angel: Aspects of Victorian Sexuality*. Women in the upper and middle classes were raised to think of themselves as decorative baubles, he points out. They sketched, played the piano, sang, constructed shell boxes, seaweed albums, and wax flowers, and embroidered cushions. "They were also, by male standards, stupid, or at least so ill-informed and intellectually circumscribed as to be reduced to a condition of stupidity," Harrison writes.

> Thus the perfectly brought-up young lady of unexceptional mental capacity represented something of a dilemma to her, let us say, equally unexceptional suitor. On the one hand, she conformed to his idea of femininity and seemed to be provided with the attributes and talents he sought in a wife; on the other, he found himself more than occasionally wearying of her conversation. Considerations of this kind seldom carry much weight with those enjoying the first, careless raptures of love, and yet the depressing discovery that his wife was dull and incapable of taking any interest in his affairs must have been made by many a husband, and must have contributed in no small way to the "leaden boredom" of many a marriage.

What the people nostalgic for Victorian domesticity had failed to grasp, I felt, was that the tensions in contemporary marriage were due not so much to a lack of commitment as to a lack of submissiveness by both men and women. What was worse—to have a marriage fraught with tension or one weighed down with "leaden boredom"?

I passed the hospital and turned down our own block. The walk through the cold night air had invigorated me, and the scenes I had witnessed through the windows had stirred me; such routine moments were the real stuff of all of our lives, I decided, and if we cherished them sufficiently our lives would be full. Our house had no stoop light, and every night, while I fumbled with the three keys I needed to get through the outer and inner doors, I told myself to attach some identifying markers—they sold rubber key caps at the newsstand—so I could distinguish them by feel in the dark, but every night I forgot that idea as soon as I entered the house, and this night was no different.

The Bialers' ancient mongrel, dying of a heart ailment, was lying in the hallway, and he feebly thumped his tail. From upstairs I heard the uncertain, interrupted notes of the piano as my daughter practiced *Heart and Soul*. I knelt to scratch the dog's head, then climbed the creaking stairs, which Stu promised to silence someday by tearing out the plaster underneath, driving wedges into the loose boards, and then replastering. At the top of the stairs I unlocked the lock on our apartment door. There had been no lock when we first moved in; we had insisted Stu install it after his son, during a wild adolescent phase now successfully negotiated, slipped in one weekend and stole a pearl necklace I had given Maureen as an anniversary present.

The kitchen, in the middle of the house, separated from the living room by a pair of white French doors, was fragrant with garlic and chicken. It was a well-lit, comforting, perpetually disheveled room. My daughter's drawings hung haphazardly on the wall. Magnets embedded in small rubber hamburgers and bagels and ice-cream sodas—all picked out by my daughter at the neighborhood curiosity shop—clamped recipes and photographs and newspaper clippings to the refrigerator door. The tables and chairs were cluttered with newspapers, schoolbooks, mail, the makings of dinner; neither my wife nor I had more than an episodic interest in tidiness, and at dinner we would sweep the accumulated papers to the back of the long pine dining table. The small television my wife kept on the counter by the microwave was tuned to a public-affairs talk show hosted by a lugubrious Canadian; tiny figures at a desk discussed the collapse of the Soviet Union. Maureen, in the middle of the well-lit kitchen, was in the act of removing the clay baking pot from the oven.

"Hello," she said in her lilting English accent.

"Hi, Dad," said my daughter, looking up from the old upright piano we bought for one hundred dollars and spent five hundred dollars to have moved and to whose yellowed ivory keys she had affixed animal stickers.

I dropped my briefcase beside the piano, hung my coat on one of the hooks I had screwed into the side panels of the hall staircase because the first floor lacked a closet, kissed first my wife and then my daughter, and as they returned to their tasks and I fixed myself a scotch I was overtaken with a feeling of pure, exultant harmony. This, the small circle of life my wife and I had created, was my own family. When I arrived, we were all complete.

Chapter 24

The problems that had driven me to leave my wife were of course still
there when I returned. But when I had been living by myself,
in that small, high-ceilinged room with the view of the dogwood
and the moss-stained brick wall, I had after a while been so overtaken by longing for my family that I became incapable of remembering why I had left except in the most vague and abstract way. I
knew I had been discontented, but the specific arguments we'd
had, and the feelings of suffocation, rage, and despair they had engendered, remained disconcertingly beyond my recall. I literally
could not summon them up; my mind would go blank when I
tried.

But while I had returned in a daze, Maureen had remained
clearheaded. She knew the problems lay buried just beneath the
surface, like the gnarled tulip bulbs we planted that fall in the
wooden flower boxes on the deck that, when the right conditions
arrived, would inevitably send up their shoots. She insisted that, if
we were going to stay together, we had to see a therapist.

The age of specialists holds out to us the hope that whatever our
problems are—our maladies and predicaments, our conundrums

and neuroses—they can be solved if we can only locate the right specialist. It is sometimes but not always a false hope. Just often enough to make believers of us all, the obscure specialist with the magic formula does indeed materialize, eradicating the crippling phobia, reversing the progress of a heretofore relentless malignancy, predicting the market's collapse. I had little enthusiasm for therapy. I had come home determined to endure my marriage but fatalistic about its condition. However, as I didn't want to appear unwilling to do anything that had a remote chance of improving our relationship—which was different, it made me sad to realize, from *wanting* to do whatever it took to make things better—I went along.

A friend of my wife's who, it surprised me to learn, was also having marriage problems, recommended her therapist, Ira Sharp. His address, on the East Side of Manhattan, presumably indicated qualifications superior to those of the neighborhood matron we had seen when I moved out.

Maureen and I began to visit Sharp once a week. I would travel up from my office. Maureen, who had gone back to work part-time, as an associate editor for *Town & Country*, would take a taxi crosstown, and we would meet in the narrow white waiting room of Sharp's office. Maureen had cut her hair that year, and it flattered her as much as the off-center ponytail she had worn when we first met. The clothes she had taken to wearing then flattered her too—long skirts, tapered French boots, white blouses, silk shawls; I never stopped admiring the way she looked. She often arrived at Sharp's office first and, when I walked in, would look up from the back issue of the *Smithsonian* or whatever other magazine she happened to be thumbing through and greet me with an expectant smile. I would exchange reserved nods with the patients waiting guardedly for the other doctors who shared the suite and sit down next to my wife. We would talk in muted tones about our daughter, and in those minutes of waiting, in that cloistered atmosphere, a sense of common endeavor would combine with the hope of therapeutic illumination to draw us together. Then Sharp's door would open and he would beckon us into his sanctuary.

Sharp was an intelligent man, rangy, with graying hair and a neat beard and a studiedly casual way of leaning back, stretching out his legs, and resting his hands on his stomach while he listened. He had a couch and two chairs, one of which was his, and to indicate hopefulness for the proceedings I always made a point of sitting next to my wife on the couch. For his benefit, we had to go over all the background once again. Sharp was the third therapist with whom I had discussed my marriage, and polishing my familiar themes and honing my anecdotes, I felt like a professional storyteller. I had my performance down cold.

Perhaps for that reason our sessions yielded little insight. The sense of common endeavor usually dissolved within the first half hour and we resorted to trading recriminations. In a misapplication of causal logic that the therapeutic process encourages, we each sought to invalidate the other's grievances by establishing prior grievances of our own, as if all subsequent wrongs could be traced to some mythic first wrong, and whoever committed it could be held responsible for everything that had transpired since.

Maureen told Sharp she thought I had a drinking problem. Since my arguments with my wife usually occurred in the evening, my wife attributed them to my drinking. I listened to my wife's references to this "pattern of drinking" and to her insistence that it was somehow linked to the problems of our marriage. I didn't buy it. Our arguments, it was true, coincided with my having a drink, but since I was gone all day, when else were we supposed to argue?

To bolster her case, Maureen would invariably point out the history of drinking in my family. Both my parents were moderate, social drinkers—a light scotch and water before dinner, a glass of wine with the meal—but I had one uncle who was a certified alcoholic. He beat his wife, stole money from his children, and couldn't keep a job; his life was full of escapades that were both hilarious and pathetic—climbing out of upper-story motel windows to escape the loan sharks banging on the door—and he died one day in his mid-fifties after blacking out, falling forward and hitting his head on the corner of a desk.

I had other uncles who could be described as either hard drinkers or functioning alcoholics. While they drank every day of their lives—going through more than a liter of scotch a week—it never interfered with the execution of their responsibilities. They lived honorably, rose early, worked hard, paid their bills, disciplined their children, treated their wives with respect. But they liked a drink or two every night. On the weekends they might start Saturday morning with a scotch and soda, polish off four or five cans of beer in the afternoon, drink so much on Saturday night they couldn't walk a straight line, and cure their Sunday-morning hangovers with Bloody Marys.

I was constitutionally incapable of such behavior. Unlike some of the journalists I had known at the newsmagazines who ritually gathered at the same saloon before lunch and again in the evening before going home, I rarely drank during the day; a glass of wine during a business lunch would leave me groggy and useless for the rest of the afternoon. I didn't go to bars. I didn't guzzle beer on the weekend. What's more, I didn't have the urge to do any of those things. I never counted the minutes until the clock hand reached the hour at which I'd promised myself I could have a drink. I even stuck to seltzer during parties because I disliked both feeling tipsy in crowds and the bleary trip home. However, I did like to have a stiff drink half an hour before dinner, a glass of wine with dinner, and then another drink before going to sleep. I thought of myself as a drinker but not a problem drinker. When I took issue with my wife's assertion, she told me I was in denial. I denied I was in denial.

Sharp, surprisingly enough, avoided taking sides on such issues. He was a pragmatist, less interested in the origins of our problems than in solutions for them. He had studied the work of a sociologist in the Pacific Northwest who had spent thousands of hours videotaping the interaction of various married couples over a dozen years and from this exhaustive fieldwork had compiled principles for successful cohabitation. Central among these were "creative communications strategies." Sharp determined that the absence of "creative communications strategies" was our problem. We both needed, he said, to learn to listen, and he gave us a book called *P.Q.R.,* which stood for Prescription for a Quality Relationship. It recommended exercises in communication and urged couples to set aside a specific time every week to practice them. In one exercise the husband and wife were both supposed to make a list of all their own bad qualities and all of their partner's virtues. The lists were to be shared. In another, each was to say "I hate you" to the other, and to repeat the phrase over and over in an increasingly loud voice until both were screaming, at which point they were to repeat the words "I love you" in a voice that decreased in volume until it was a whisper.

We gamely tried a couple of these exercises—not the "hate you," "love you" chant—on Saturday mornings while Jessica played at a friend's house. But they made me feel self-conscious and foolish. The notion that relationships could be untangled by such reductive and schematic formulas, I thought, underestimated human complexity. Life was more mysterious than this! But the book, with its royal-blue jacket and gold-lettered title and punchy exhortations, also saddened me. Other people had taken it to heart. It represented hope to them, and presumably some of them had used it to good effect. That my wife and I failed to get anything out of the book, which, after our few halfhearted efforts to plumb its wisdom, ended up on a remote shelf in the upstairs study, indicated that our problem was not that we needed to "learn" how to communicate but that at some point, it was impossible to say just when, we had lost the desire to do so.

The therapy began to lose momentum. In February, after a particularly stagnant session, Sharp looked at the two of us and said, "You're one of the most low-energy couples I've ever treated."

At first I felt insulted. I didn't think of myself as a low-energy person. I thought I bristled with energy—at times anyway. But Sharp was right. Individually we may have registered some wattage, but when it came to our marriage, neither of us cared enough any longer to make an effort. We *were* low-energy, and this realization sapped me even further. By the spring the therapy had stalled completely, and we stopped seeing Sharp. Even with the insurance copayment the sessions were expensive. And besides, Maureen and I agreed, there just wasn't any point. We had reached what I, depending on my state of mind, would think of as an impasse, a stalemate, or a truce.

Alex called one day that winter to suggest we have lunch. It had been more than a year since we had last seen each other. We met the following week in a paneled restaurant with sepia photographs of Venetian canals on the stretched-fabric walls and linen-draped tables so small they seemed to have been designed for children. Alex, wearing a cream-colored dress and a single strand of pearls, was already there when I arrived. I thought she looked sensational. Both the jewelry and the outfit underscored the glow of her burnished skin. She had always dressed well, but now her clothing seemed elegant instead of merely expensive. She had cropped her hair extremely short, which accentuated her worldliness. It made her seem more interesting and mature, more intelligent and poised, and it sharpened her already considerable sexual aura.

"I was getting too old for long hair," she told me. "It had stopped making me look younger and instead was making me look like someone trying to look younger."

Alex ordered two of the pretentious champagne cocktails that were the specialty of the house. The meal, she said, was her treat; the previous October she had been promoted into the senior management of her firm. I began to congratulate her, but she restrained me. The purpose of the lunch, she said, was not to celebrate her new job. It was to celebrate her engagement. The news surprised, pleased, and relieved me. I had disappointed her and had worried that the subsequent men in her life, alarmed by her intentionality, might do the same. But it also made me jealous; I had imagined I was irreplaceable.

"So who is he?" I asked.

He was the head of his own executive search firm, she said. The first time she saw him, across the crowded room at a reception, she felt an immediate attraction and had walked over and introduced herself. He was a "real man," she said, unlike so many of the emotionally stunted "boys" she had dated, boys afraid of commitment and uncomfortable with the female urge toward emotional connection, boys who wanted sex but were terrified of the strength of awakened female desire. Her fiancé was powerful and authoritative, she said. Executive recruitment was his second career. Before that, he'd spent twenty years in the FBI, ending up as the deputy director for human resources.

He was also a widower, she added as she took a set of photographs from her purse. And he was older than she was. But he was mad about her. Their lovemaking was so frantic, she said, it seemed at times insane. He told her that she had given him a new lease on life, that with her he felt regenerated. She was the reward he had worked for his entire life, he told her, and he wanted to give her a child.

"Here we are on Block Island," she said. She passed over a photograph in which she stood on a dock arm in arm with a man whose rectangular glasses, receding gray hair, and leathery jowls suggested to me that he was, at the least, in his mid-sixties.

"I said he was older." She searched my face for my reaction.

"How much older?"

"He's sixty-seven." She paused. "What do you think?"

"Well," I said, "he looks like a nice guy."

It was a vacuous comment, I knew, but it was the best I could muster. Tears crowded into Alex's eyes.

"What am I supposed to do?" she cried.

I understood her question perfectly; we all have far fewer options than we like to imagine.

Chapter 25

"Ed and Meg have split up," my wife said.

"But they've been together since high school."

"I know."

Ed and Meg Hennessee lived six blocks away. He was a polite, dapper man who'd had a precarious career on Wall Street, moving from firm to firm in the quest for an elusive partnership. Meg, broad-shouldered, with freckles and a blunt nose, taught in a private school. Her practical haircut, plain clothes, and disdain for makeup made me think of her as the quintessential mom. Whatever other attributes her identity may have encompassed, they were submerged within the maternal.

Ed and Meg had four children, a family so unusually large by the standards of the neighborhood that it was as if they practiced some archaic religion. They had started dating as teenagers and had married immediately after college. Neither had ever been involved with anyone else. It was a rare accomplishment, one that, like the size of their family, made them appear charmingly innocent but at the same time freakish. They had, I thought, warded off all the temptations of the modern world and lived steeped in domestic contentment. We had spent evenings at their house eating fried fish and drinking California wine and discussing local real estate while our children charged up and down the stairs in a game of hide-and-seek. I wondered what impulsive restlessness had driven them—in their forties, with a teenage son and three younger daughters in private school, with complicated finances and a long peaceful history together—to split up.

One night a couple of weeks later, walking home along the neighborhood's main avenue, I ran into Meg. Her hair was wet and she carried a gym bag. She had just come, she said, from a swim at the Y, and she gave me the impression this was a new freedom she had discovered, a solitary luxury unavailable to her during her marriage. I was sorry, I said, to hear she and Ed were separating.

"You'd been together since high school," I couldn't help adding.

She nodded, pushed back her wet hair, and said, "That was part of the problem."

What exactly do you accomplish by staying married to one person for your entire life? One of my aunts, an affectionate, opinionated widow who supported herself making Christmas ornaments from flour dough, liked to talk about the terrible fights she and her late husband used to have. If they had allowed those fights to affect them, she was fond of saying, they would never have stayed married. But despite the ferocious fights, neither of them seriously considered ending the marriage. Why not? I wondered. Why do we value commitment so highly? What's the point?

There are practical considerations, and children are primary among them. But even without children, it is cheaper to remain married. If the couple breaks up, both husband and wife usually suffer a drop in living standards, and while many husbands recover, their wives are often permanently impoverished. Fear of loneliness is another practical consideration; couples stay with each other out of the same instinct that propels buffalo to herd together during a storm. Commitment also offers the prospect of a shared peace in old age. There is the idea, a sentimental one but in many cases borne out, that if a couple can endure the rough spells they will not regret it, and together will enjoy an old age enriched by their pool of shared memories.

But such considerations still render marriage conditional. They are rationales. By suggesting it is in the interests of a couple to remain married, they imply that both partners can and should determine what their individual interests are and therefore whether their particular marriage serves those interests. Some couples, even when they have nothing in common and practical considerations would seem to argue against it, remain married only to set an example for their children, to prove that it can be done.

Why, I began to wonder, do we treat matrimonial endurance as the ideal to which, even if we fail, we should aspire? Is there a reason—aside from blind adherence to Christ's admonition that "Those whom God hath joined together let no man put asunder"—why a life lived with one mate is morally superior to "consecutive polygamy"? In researching this question, I came across the work of Hermann Keyserling, a German count and writer who made what could be called the "existential" argument for commitment.

Keyserling, writing in the twenties, called marriage "a state of tragic tension." The tension and the tragedy derived, he believed, from the fact that marriage encompassed irreconcilable conflicts—conflicts between, for example, self-interest and duty, or freedom and responsibility. "Marriage acquires its true meaning only when the partnership is based on the realization of its tragic significance," Keyserling wrote. He went on to say, "The fulfillment of marriage and its happiness entail the acceptance of the suffering pertaining to life. It gives the latter a new and deeper meaning. . . . But whoever accepts the suffering from the outset places himself in the very center of the meaning of life."

In Keyserling's view, the man or woman who fled an unhappy marriage was trying to evade the very meaning of existence. Accepting the disappointments of marriage was a way of beginning to accept the disappointments of life, the suffering it entailed, and the death that ended it. At first I found this line of reasoning compelling. Our dissatisfaction with marriage is narcissistic, Keyserling seemed to be saying. We reject marriage because it was impossible, within the intimacy it created, to maintain our idealized view of ourselves. We hated our wives and husbands because they came to know our weaknesses and forced us to acknowledge them. Recoiling from that intimacy, we sought out new lovers with whom we could reinvent ourselves, lovers who would for a while, until they got to know us, subscribe to our idealized view of ourselves. Marriage, as Keyserling sees it, forces us to confront who we are.

But after a while I began to feel uneasy with the pessimistic assumptions behind Keyserling's idea of "tragic tension." The notion that we ought to embrace suffering came to seem morbidly Teutonic. Was it really narcissistic and escapist to try to avoid suffering, to arrange our affairs so that our brief existence is as pleasant and enjoyable as possible? And wasn't it possible to view marriages as organic? Some, it seems, have a brief duration; others last a decade or two; still others, like great hardwoods, seem to have no fixed life span at all. But they are all living and a number of them do die out. Are we to stay in dead marriages as the best way to prepare ourselves for the day when we too will be dead?

It was the end of Ed and Meg's marriage that made me realize that I could no longer think of the divorces among these friends and acquaintances as isolated instances of malfunction. Some sort of collective collapse seemed to be occurring, a gradual disintegration of the social order that was, as the death of the Roman Empire was to the Europeans of the early Middle Ages, scarcely perceptible to those living through it. But it was scattering the community—with its opinionated mothers in sweatpants, its herds of children, its husbands who spent the weekends, unless they took the children to the playground, fetishistically restoring their old brownstones—we had discovered when we moved to the neighborhood.

Shortly after Ed and Meg separated, my wife and I learned that Syd and Lois, our neighbors across the street, were splitting up. Syd had begun seeing another woman, an attractive but sullen nineteen-year-old African American, and in keeping with their policy of an "open marriage," he had informed his wife about the affair. Lois had never been enthusiastic about the policy, she later told my wife, but since she had three children, she had gone along with it as a way of keeping the family together. Now, after twenty years together, she had tired of the arrangement. The family was dissolving, anyway, as the children grew up and moved out—the formal dining room that they had converted into a bedroom, pushing a desk against the carved mahogany fireplace and taping animal posters to the beveled mirrors, now stood empty—and she saw no point in continuing to live this way. She balked at the affair. Syd, perhaps seizing an opportunity he had long been waiting for, moved out into a tiny apartment four blocks away, which he furnished with a few cast-off pieces he found in his basement.

I ran into him in front of the house one Saturday morning a couple of weeks after he had moved out. It was early summer. He had just finished pruning his juneberry tree and was carrying a rusty hacksaw. He had cut his graying hair short and exchanged his heavy plastic-framed glasses for wire rims. He looked leaner, more chiseled, and he professed to be completely happy with his new situation.

"I don't have anyone bothering me," he said. "All my life—I grew up in a large family, I worked on a shop floor, I started a large family of my own—I've had people bothering me. They're in my face, they're acting out, they want help with something—I've always had to be on, to relate. Now, I lie on my bed in my room, and I stare at the ceiling, and I've got no one to think about and nothing to worry about."

I found this incomprehensible. I too, when I had moved out, had lain on a bed, hands tucked behind my head, all alone in a tiny apartment, and stared at the ceiling. But it brought me no relief or peace. I felt I had locked myself out of my own house, and I longed to get back in. To me the family, that structure of reciprocal obligation reinforced by minor daily ceremony, was where I discovered my identity. The fact that my wife and I didn't get along, I had convinced myself, no longer mattered. We were a family. We had made a commitment. And it was our daughter that made us a family.

I couldn't imagine life without my daughter. She was nine then, with long blond hair, her mother's almond-shaped eyes, and my sudden moods. Her walk had recently assumed a coltish litheness, and she showed the first smoky glimmerings of a hidden inner life; we had taken her to see *Phantom of the Opera,* and she liked now to sit by herself in the living room listening to the music, dreaming of gilded prisons and underground rivers, madmen and masked lovers. But she was still a kid. In her room she had four plastic boxes filled with Barbies whose hair she had, for her own unfathomable reasons, cropped. She kept a herd of Breyer horses under her bed in a stable she had built from cardboard. A ridiculously excessive pile of stuffed animals—bears with oatmeal-colored fur, long-haired cats, floppy-eared dogs, a crimson parrot from Cuba, two lime-green alligators with mouths that zippered shut—were crammed onto the shelves above her desk. At night she and I would turn off all her lights and sit at her bay window watching people move about in the lit rooms on the far side of the enclosed gardens and speculate about their lives. Then I would tuck her into bed, pull up the cotton duvet with its pattern of tiny rabbits, and lie down beside her, under the faint glow of the phosphorescent plastic stars we had fixed to the ceiling, the air pump for the aquarium I had bought her bubbling and humming in the darkness, and invent adventure stories about a nine-year-old girl named Jessica. What did it matter whether my wife and I got along if every day had moments like those? What could the world possibly offer me in exchange for them? How could any father not feel the same?

So I didn't believe Syd when he told me how happy he was by himself in his small new apartment. I thought he was trying to convince himself by convincing me, just as he had years earlier when, with his wife away for the weekend with her lover, he had explained how their open marriage worked. But maybe this was a failure of imagination on my part. Maybe it was true. Maybe Syd was a social man who had always dreamed of solitude just as I was a loner who yearned to be the life of the party. We all long for our opposites; we all carry within us irreconcilable contradictions.

Chapter 26

I was writing a weekly political column in those days. The job provided me with my own office, a small television set on which I could watch the press conferences and political speeches that coincided with deadlines, and a part-time assistant who treated every request I made as an outrageous imposition. When I began the column, an apartment building was under construction across the street, and the first time I opened the window in my office the cacophonous din from the site reminded me of the occasion, years earlier, when the supervisor at the first newsmagazine I had worked for had called me into his office and, over an identical barrage of noise, told me he thought I had exhausted my luck there. Several years later he too was pushed out of the company, but when I ran into him at a restaurant sometime afterward, I resisted the temptation to point out that he seemed to have exhausted his luck there as well, and merely waved. He had, after all, been right.

My father, always more at home in the world of ideas, thought I had the most enviable job in the world. It *was* enviable, but there was also, for a constitutionally ambivalent person like myself, something frighteningly relentless and at times even oppressive about the daily manufacture of opinion. A foot-high stack of newspapers awaited me on my desk when I arrived at my office each morning: *The New York Times,* the *New York Post,* the *Daily News, Newsday, The Washington Post, The Boston Globe, The Wall Street Journal,* the *Los Angeles Times, USA Today.* And if it was Monday, on top of the newspapers would be a smaller stack of magazines: *Time, Newsweek, U.S. News & World Report, The Nation, The New Republic,* and *The New Yorker,* plus whatever other publications——*The National Review, The National Journal, Commentary*——and policy studies had arrived in the mail. I would hang my suit jacket on the hook behind the door——the job seemed to require a suit, though no one said so—— uncap my cup of scalding takeout coffee, and dive into this vast compendium of human confusion. Deficit reduction, school vouchers, welfare reform, Clinton's chances in Texas, Palestinian autonomy, racial preferences, mandatory sentencing, Giuliani's chances in Queens, illegal immigration, casino gambling, soft money, the flat tax, federal mining subsidies——it was not enough to simply have an opinion on these matters. That was the easy part. The opinion needed to be both passionately felt and irreproachably authoritative.

But I enjoyed my work. I had one essential ingredient for a columnist: a perverse desire to counter prevailing opinion. And the job kept me busy. If it was Monday I had until the middle of the afternoon to decide what I was going to write about that week. If it required traveling, and it usually did——I had joined the frequent flyer programs of seven airlines——I would have to leave the city that evening or early the following morning; report and write the piece, from Richmond or St. Louis or Washington or Miami, on Tuesday and Wednesday; and relay it by modem back to the office on Thursday morning, inserting the phone line in my hotel room into the back of the laptop, dialing, listening to the rhapsodic screeches and chirps, the ecstasies of electronic transmission, as my computer conjoined with the office mainframe, and the scrolled wisps of my writing spiraled through the fiber-optic cables.

I would then fly back to the city, come into the office, and close the column. On Friday I caught up on my reading—the stack of newspapers on my desk would grow precariously high if I was away for more than a couple of days; my thumbs would turn carbon-black and cramp up after leafing through the thousands of pages of newsprint—occasionally appeared on local television, and planned the next week.

A couple of years passed in this fashion. It was not, I had to admit, a bad life in many respects. I traveled, earned a respectable salary, met influential people, and since I was, if not at the top, near the top of my profession, I even enjoyed a modest degree of influence myself. The weeks, crowded with hectic days, with appointments and interviews and decisions and deadlines, had a swift galloping pace. I was living what I thought was universally acknowledged to be a fully realized existence at the close of the twentieth century. Under pressure and in demand, hurrying through another mall-like airport with a scuffed tan garment bag slung over one shoulder, the laptop, in its black canvas satchel, hanging from my other shoulder and banging ponderously against my hip, and in my hand a worn leather briefcase thick with unread policy analyses, unreturned phone messages taken by my ungrateful assistant, and unfiled expense-account receipts, I had achieved the condition—of complete immersion in my historical moment—to which we were all supposed to aspire.

In addition, I had the satisfying sense that I was fulfilling my responsibilities. I paid the Master Card and the Visa and the American Express bills, the Con Ed and the Brooklyn Union Gas and the New York Telephone bills. I paid the AT&T bill, with my wife's long-distance calls to her sister and parents in London. I gave my wife cash and I paid my daughter's shockingly steep and sneakily increasing school tuition, and I paid for the maid who came every other week, though I wasn't sure why, since my wife was no longer working—her department at *Town & Country* had been closed in an episode of early-nineties downsizing—we needed a maid. I also didn't know exactly what it was my wife did with her days. I knew she saw friends. I knew she shopped for food and talked on the phone and read Anita Brookner and Sue Miller and *Mirabella*. I knew that, from some impulse of feminist defiance, she refused to wash my clothes when she washed her own and our daughter's, leaving me to do my own laundry on the weekends. But I tried not to complain. I tried to encourage my wife to get a job, for her own sake, and I know there was at times a note of exasperation and disbelief in my voice when I told her I disagreed with her insistence that there was no work out there, but I tried not to complain. I tried not to complain about anything.

I had by then become involved with someone else and had begun to accept the fact that I was destined to have what I thought of as a European marriage: one wife; serial mistresses. This, I told myself, was how the English and the French, the Italians and the Mexicans and the Brazilians, all did it. Inheritors of the tradition of the arranged marriage, a contract designed to provide not lifelong psychospiritual intimacy but economic security and legitimate heirs, they had a much less romantic view of human sexuality. They accepted the possibility that sexual attraction existed outside marriage and they tolerated and even encouraged it, realizing that the fewer demands a marriage had to satisfy, the more likely it was to endure.

Sheryl Gates, the woman I had become involved with, was also married and was prepared to remain that way for the rest of her life. Her husband, a self-absorbed tax lawyer, worked most evenings until ten or eleven and returned to the office on weekends. He had no interest in having children except under an arrangement that officially absolved him from any responsibility in raising them; he calculated, he once told his wife, that he could af-

ford to spend a maximum of only three hours a week with a child
if she wanted to have one. Despite the almost pathological nar-
rowness of his interests, he was a civilized, courteous man. He
loved his wife in his fashion and treated her well, and the two of
them lived a privileged if emotionally barren existence in a large
Riverside Drive apartment—ceiling beams, herringbone floorboards, an elevator paneled in cherrywood—that he had inherited
from his mother. Sheryl had grown up in an impoverished Appalachian mining town, not too far north of Lone Mountain, with
a drunken father and a semicataleptic mother—she and her
brother had often been forced to walk the railroad tracks searching for stray pieces of coal to heat the two-room shack they all
lived in—and she was grateful to her husband for the security he
provided her. It was, in fact, the reason she had married him. She
no longer required security. She now had her own career and an
income that would have astounded her coal-streaked neighbors in
West Virginia. But she believed she owed a debt to her husband for
giving her what she needed when she needed it.

The obligations we both felt—Sheryl to her husband, me to
my wife—created a balance in our relationship. Neither of us
pushed the other for anything. Neither made demands, applied
pressure, or delivered ultimatums, and as a result, without the
claustrophobic weight of frustrated expectations, we became re-
markably close. We met most Thursday nights at a hotel near my
office, a clean, reasonable place where the staff, who came to expect us, treated us affectionately, and afterward had dinner at an
Italian restaurant across the street. It had not been redecorated
since the sixties and its tinkling fountain and heavy ornate chairs
gave it a musty period air, but its staff, who also came to expect us,
treated us like royalty. Seeing us together made waiters, clerks,
coat-check girls, and taxi drivers smile. People we knew professionally assumed we were having an affair, and as I eventually
learned, we were the subject of a considerable amount of gossip,

but since our relationship was semipublic, and since I felt bracingly unapologetic about it, none of that bothered me. Or her.

I thought I had solved the problem, come upon the arrangement that would provide everyone—my wife, Sheryl, my daughter, myself—with more of what we needed than either divorce or fidelity or, God forbid, continued therapy. It was far from perfect. It meant accepting a lie in the core of your life, but that was easier to do than I thought. It involved no greater deception than living in a loveless marriage. The only difference was that, instead of deceiving yourself, you were deceiving someone else. There was, I felt, an urbane Continental quality to the hypocrisy it entailed. Hypocrisy is always logical, after all, a rational response to contradictory imperatives; civilization would collapse without it. I thought, with some self-dramatization, of Graham Greene and Catherine Walston, Ernest Hemingway and Jane Mason, Spencer Tracy and Katharine Hepburn. They had all tried to balance the competing claims of passion and duty without surrendering entirely to either. Their solutions were unconventional and not wholly satisfactory; while Walston was happy to invite Greene to her house and to make love behind the altars of Italian churches, she refused to leave her husband for him. But didn't that just mean that these affairs, as Keyserling said of marriage itself, encompassed irreconcilable conflicts? And didn't that mean that, like marriage itself, such affairs existed in "a state of tragic tension" and thus placed us, in Keyserling's phrase, at "the very center of the meaning of life"?

Chapter 27

If moral authenticity is a fiction, why do we yearn for it? If the desire for truth is culturally conditioned, the product of upbringing and perhaps genetic predisposition, can it nonetheless be so deeply ingrained in our beings that dishonesty literally sickens us?

I thought I had fashioned a coherent moral framework for my life. I was aware of the potential it afforded me to justify what could be considered contemptible behavior, but I had satisfied myself, anyway, on that point. Self-justification was not an issue. I knew that my hand-tailored morality involved compromises. I accepted them and was prepared to bear their consequences.

Primary among these, it turned out, was a chronic sense of emotional imbalance, of internal misalignment. As my wife and I, in our periodic discussions, thrashed through the early days of our marriage, trying to isolate the turning point, I realized that there were so many things about our relationship that I couldn't remember. Who had proposed? Where? What had our first argument been about? When had it taken place? I couldn't say. I slowly became aware that a fog, a sodden occluding vapor, had settled over my mind. I felt dull and inadequate. My intellectual responses were slow to flare.

The irritability that had provoked me to gestures of stupid violence had never subsided. To the contrary, in those later years it had sharpened. I felt peevish, wired, and negative, easily startled and quickly disgusted. I had also, it surprised me to realize, developed an abiding revulsion for the city in which I lived. The garbage trucks from the Sanitation Department, which picked up trash one day, recycled paper a second, and recycled bottles a third, usually reached our street by eight o'clock in the morning. The grinding of the truck's compactor, the honking of the cars delayed behind the truck as it worked its way up the block, and the mad shrieks of car alarms touched off when the garbage collectors carelessly tossed emptied trash cans against parked vehicles all combined to produce a stunning din. Every morning, it seemed, began with the infernal, abominable noise of the metropolis.

And then there was the trash. Vagrants in search of returnable bottles and cans had taken to splitting apart the plastic trash bags merchants set out at night and spilling the contents onto the sidewalks. Litter and refuse swirled through the streets of our neighborhood like postapocalyptic debris. When I walked Jessica to her school we had to wade through a knee-high tide of stained discarded packaging and wind-tossed newsprint.

The neighborhood, which had seemed so serene when we first moved there, now had a wolfish, menacing atmosphere. The Bialers, below us, were burglarized at least once a summer for three years running. One night, when Mattie woke up and went into the living room, two men were removing the television; they told her to sit down on the couch and stay quiet until they were gone. On another afternoon she came home to find that burglars using a hydraulic automobile jack had effortlessly pried apart the iron bars on the garden-level windows and slipped into the house to make off with whatever appliances the previous burglars had neglected to take. The crime reports in the local papers carried stories of schoolchildren sexually assaulted *in the schools* by predators who had evaded the security guards and metal detectors in place at every entrance.

Even my morning walk with Jessica had become fraught with danger. Although now, at age ten, she tended to be disdainful of holding my hand, she instinctively clutched it when we passed the neighborhood's notorious and overcrowded public high school, where the herds of students in baggy, flapping jeans, with nicknames and merchandise logos razored into their cropped hair, lounged on car hoods smoking cigarettes and talking in obscenity-larded sentences. One morning, less than a block from her school, we found the street closed off by a police cordon. Yellow tape, whirling lights, the crackle of walkie-talkies. Only minutes earlier, one of the bystanders told me, gunmen had tried to rob a bank branch on the street corner, and when the police arrived, summoned by a silent alarm, a shoot-out had occurred. Bullets had sprayed the street, shattering storefront glass, sending pedestrians diving for cover. A shoot-out! At eight-thirty in the morning! Half a block from my daughter's school!

Maybe all of these things took on exaggerated significance. Perhaps I was guilty of a pathetic fallacy, of attributing to the scene the sentiments of the viewer. My neighbors seemed oblivious to the blight; they walked through the knee-high trash as if it were invisible. The neighborhood had always been slightly seedy and dangerous; that accounted for a good portion of its urban appeal. It redeemed it from the purely charming. Still, I now hated the place I had once loved so much. The litter, the noise, and the violence didn't just annoy me, they tormented me. I felt persecuted, trapped in a life not, I felt, of my own making, in a city I had come to despise.

Nonetheless, I had determined that I wasn't going to leave my wife. I had left her once and returned, and in doing so I felt I had forfeited the right to depart again. What I didn't realize during those years was the extent to which Maureen was also experiencing a sense of internal misalignment. In my stoic and dutiful approach to our marriage, I was depriving her of any true companionship, and eleven and a half years after our wedding it had become intolerable to her.

"We have to separate," my wife said again on that late-summer day when we sat on the deck drinking gin-and-tonics and smoking cigarettes while the sun set behind the Victorian schoolhouse.

She had swept us forward to a moment I had both dreaded and longed for. The plunge through the darkness had stopped, the encrusted mechanism of our marriage had finally sprung apart.

I looked across our yard. The sun had slid behind the slate mansard roof of the elementary school, veiling the surrounding gardens with their birch trees and weeping cherry trees and tangled rosebushes in a dusty, golden light. The basketball game had stopped. The ensuing tranquillity felt dense, almost palpable. From deep within it could be heard the city's faint incessant rumble.

I remember each moment of that conversation distinctly. I remember rattling the ice in my second gin and lighting another cigarette. I remember my senses feeling constricted by the enormity of what we were discussing. I remember looking through the screen door and seeing my daughter, her head in profile, an image of innocent absorption as she sat at the dining table finishing her homework and humming in a loud tuneless voice.

It's been said that to stay together for the sake of the children, which has been the choice of many couples, burdens those children with the responsibility for their parents' unhappiness. It's been said too that to separate for the sake of the children, a less frequent rationalization but one that has also from time to time been invoked, makes them responsible for their own abandonment. It's been said that parents avoid taking responsibility for their own lives by claiming to act "for the sake of the children," and of course it's been said that to ignore the interests of the children is the height of immorality.

For years my wife and I had talked between ourselves, with therapists, with friends, with family, about "what would be best" for our daughter. We were sure our separation would be traumatic for her. I worried about this, I think, more than my wife did. Every child's greatest fear—greater than the fear of death, since most children don't believe in the possibility of their own death—is the fear of abandonment. That, at least, was my own conviction. Sitting on the deck, I remembered how such a fear swept through me when I was a child and my mother was late picking me up from some appointment, leaving me standing on a street corner for half an hour. For me at Jessica's age, the prospect of my own parents separating was something I literally would have been unable to imagine.

While she agreed that a separation would be traumatic for our daughter, my wife was unsure how enduring the trauma would be, and even less sure how healthy it would be for her to grow up in a lifeless marriage. She worried, more than I did, about the effect of our unhappiness on our daughter. Jessica, it was true, had become exquisitely attuned to intimations of discord. At the first note of tension tightening in our voices, she would warn, "Don't fight! Don't fight!" If we separated, my daughter would stay with my wife. The thought of living without her paralyzed me. What role could I play in her life if I saw her only on Wednesday nights and alternate weekends? To be a real father, I was convinced, you had to be there at the moments of crisis or discovery:

when it occurred to her to ask how fish lived underwater, when the math problem stymied her, when her finger got caught in the car door.

"I don't think I can go through with it," I said.

"We *have* to."

Why? I wondered. For all our problems, we managed the logistics of our lives: took our daughter to the dentist, paid the bills, planned the holiday travel schedule. We had evolved a complex avoidance system. The morning, always a rush, provided little opportunity for discord. When I returned in the evening I had my drink and helped my daughter with her homework while my wife made dinner. After dinner I washed the dishes while my wife watched TV in our bedroom, then I read and nursed another drink downstairs until she turned off the lights. Often I slept in the living room, a development my daughter accepted with mild, easily appeased curiosity. ("I don't want to catch Mommy's cold.") On weekends we went our separate ways, with me taking my daughter skiing, skating, or swimming one day, then spending the long afternoon of the next at the gym while she and my wife went to the movies or a museum.

What this meant was that we had already separated, with an elaborate if unacknowledged joint-custody agreement, but just happened to be occupying the same household. Is this it? I often asked myself, lying on my makeshift bed on the living-room floor. Upstairs, my wife was asking herself the same question. And this *was* it. My wife and I both lacked the will to improve our marriage. We could either endure it or end it.

Facing divorce means answering the question: I have one life, it's extremely short, how do I want to live it? My wife, with fewer options than I had outside our marriage, felt more urgently than I did the need to free herself from its confines. She was stronger than I was, I realized that summer evening, more self-reliant. She had greater inner resources and clarity of vision. I had believed I was staying married, in large part, out of a sense of duty to my wife, an obligation to stay with her in sickness and in health. But I saw, as the twilight settled over our neighborhood, that despite her medical condition she did not need me as much as I thought she did. My real obligation was to set her free. In exchange, if I left, she would absolve me of my guilt.

Chapter 28

A couple of weeks later I had what my wife later referred to as "the panic attack." It was late in the evening. Our daughter was asleep, and we had been in our bedroom discussing the impending separation. I was once again unsure of what to do. I became so distressed by the conversation—by the idea that through an act of volition I was going to destroy the world that my wife and daughter and I had formed, the world I had inhabited for twelve years, the only world my daughter had ever known—that I went down to the kitchen, poured some ice and vodka into a coffee mug, then sat out on the deck smoking and drinking, and watching through the windows of the house next door as my neighbor, the father of newborn twins, washed the dishes.

The sight reminded me of that night I had walked home through the snowstorm and, looking through the windows of the houses I passed, had felt for a moment unsurpassed contentment with the routine of my own life. It hadn't lasted long. To be able to accept and love the ordinariness of existence—as my neighbor, patiently soaping his plates, seemed to be doing—is a great gift, one I wished I could claim. I wondered if it was a superficial longing for drama that had led me to manufacture problems in my life that might otherwise never have existed or if they had existed would have proved surmountable. I became convinced that this was true, that it was my inability to resist temptation, my desire for an "interesting" and "exciting" life, that had ruined my marriage. I had failed the test, I realized. I was weak, selfish, and shallow, a man without character.

I was, I admit, drinking too heavily during those weeks. That night I had had a couple of drinks before dinner and wine with dinner, and out on the deck, when I finished the cigarette and stood up, I realized I was drunk. It didn't alarm me. I had been in this position before, though not often and not recently. I went upstairs and lay down in bed next to my sleeping wife. I was still agitated by the conviction that I had failed her and my daughter. I looked at the ceilings and walls, just visible in the faint yellow streetlight that filtered in around the edges of the navy flowered curtains my wife had made when we first moved in. Instead of soothing me with their solid planes they shifted and folded, pleating, and I felt a sliding sensation, as if the surface of the bed were tipping.

I tried to calm myself, but I couldn't. My mind began to spiral and then tumble, revolving around itself. The rush of dizziness was instantaneous and sickening. In a panic, I called out to my wife, waking her. She tried to quiet me, worried that I might wake our daughter and touch off who knew what terrors, but she failed. *My mind's spinning,* I cried out, *I can't make it stop.* Thoroughly frightened, my wife called 911 and some twenty minutes later we heard the sound of the siren. I had heard thousands of sirens in my years in the city. One was finally coming for me. The doorbell rang. My wife led two EMS technicians into our bedroom. The men, invading the bedroom, seemed to fill it. Their presence was massive. Privacy is so frail, so easily violated. I lay there, ridiculous and vulnerable in my underwear, while they took my blood pressure and spoke to each other in bored conversational tones.

My wife insisted they take me to the hospital. I remember their helping me down the stairs, each of them holding an elbow.

Their boots thudded dangerously, as if forged from iron, on either side of my feet. The staircase, which our landlord had never fixed, groaned under our combined weight. In the ambulance I sat in the back, and they sat up front and continued their bored conversation. Their lack of interest in me, their patient, was impressive. At the hospital the admitting nurse told me no doctor was immediately free to examine me. But I was already feeling better. I lay down on a stretcher, and in a matter of minutes my head had cleared. The moral confusion that had engulfed me on the deck had subsided completely. I felt tired and calm. I got up and walked home. It was only half a block away.

The next day I dismissed the episode. I had been under pressure and had had a little too much to drink; these things happen. My wife, however, was convinced that it was a sign of how serious my drinking problem had become. That night she demanded that I stop drinking. I refused. Why should I? I asked. I'd never needed— or, I felt, deserved—a drink more than I did during those days. My wife said she was leaving the house and taking my daughter. She had become afraid of me, she said, afraid that I might have another attack, that I might this time become violent instead of panicked, that our daughter might somehow be exposed to my derangement, with God knew what consequences.

Maureen packed a bag and went to stay with friends, two doctors who had a daughter Jessica's age and who lived in a brick town house too large for them on the busy avenue behind the hospital. After dinner Jeffrey, the husband, came around to see how I was doing, and we sat out on the deck, in the dark, smoking cigarettes and drinking wine. Jeffrey was British, the chief of medicine at a large inner-city hospital. My wife and I had known him and his wife, an Israeli psychiatrist, since our daughters were small. We had enjoyed memorable, wonderful times together: cookouts at

the beach; dinners in hectic Russian restaurants; Passover celebra-
tions in our kitchen; recitals in the grim apartment of the shy, thin
woman who taught both our daughters piano; heated debates,
while sitting late at night in the tiny wall-enclosed garden behind
their house, about the invasion of Iraq and the merits of recovered
memories. Jeffrey was zestful and sardonic, his wife animated and
bossy. We all loved a good argument, and even though his wife's
faith in recovered memories incensed me and my support for the
Palestinians drew her scorn, none of us ever lost our temper during those late-night debates. None of us ever said anything we re-
gretted. They were two of our closest friends.

But as Jeffrey's hospital had sunk into insolvency, with
chronic shortages of everything from soap to toilet paper, and our
marriage foundered, we had become preoccupied with our individual problems and drifted apart. An abiding fatigue had worked
its way into his spirit, I saw that night. He seemed chronically
weary. His wife and daughter were both talented but difficult, and
I'd always had the sense that much of his marriage was a grueling
slog. As we sat out on the deck he admitted that it was. But divorce, he said, was out of the question. He simply could not conceive of living apart from his daughter. He may have been weary,
he said, but he hadn't surrendered. The fact that in his mind I had
done so made me, I could see, incomprehensible to him.

We were two men on the verge of middle age, realizing just
how much of our lives were already unrecoverable, but we'd each
made our decisions and they had moved us in opposite directions.
We didn't have that much to say to each other, and after we finished the bottle of wine Jeffrey left. I saw him once after that, at
the annual piano recital, but we spoke only briefly, and then I
heard from my wife that he had given up on the decrepit hospital
that had taken so much of his life and accepted a job with an HMO
in Hartford. In the end, and in his own way, he too, I came to feel,
had surrendered.

When Maureen returned after one night with Jeffrey and his wife, her mind was made up. The time for me to go had come. The "panic attack," which foretold to her a future of irrational violence unless she took action, proved to be the decisive incident. It took me a few weeks to finally accept the idea and then a few more weeks to work up the will to begin looking for an apartment. I found one only a block away, but that, I felt, was too close. I found another, with leaded windows framing a handsome view of the stone steeple of a Presbyterian church, but I would have had to move out in two years. I didn't want to be in that position. A third had no light, a fourth was too small. If I was going to be living by myself for the first time in fourteen years, it needed to be in a place that wouldn't push me over the edge. It was not enough for the apartment to be satisfactory on balance, with advantages and disadvantages, or even good, with the advantages outweighing the disadvantages. It had to be perfect. I continued looking. Meanwhile, time passed.

Chapter 29

W"e should see a mediator," Maureen said. *She sat at our kitchen* table, a cup of herbal tea and her black Filofax in front of her. Now that we had resolved to split up, she was acting with decisiveness and energy.

I agreed with the idea; the prospect of divorce lawyers draining our negligible assets as they fought over them terrified me.

Maureen said she already had the name of a mediator, Howard Yahm, who, to the satisfaction of all parties, had negotiated the divorce settlement of a friend of a friend. "Shall I call him?" she asked.

I stifled an urge to open the whole matter up for reconsideration and nodded. Maureen put on the reading glasses she had recently taken to wearing and opened her Filofax. The portable phone stood on the piano, next to a drawing from Jessica's Matisse period. I passed it to Maureen. Yahm agreed to see us, she made an appointment, and two weeks later, on an unseasonably brisk September day, we met in his office on the Upper West Side.

Yahm was a small, almost gnomish man with a ponytail and a wild gray beard. He wore a heavy knitted sweater, jeans, and mountain boots with red laces. His office had two large windows overlooking an elementary school playground, a bookcase filled with psychology texts, and a cluttered desk. On one wall was a photograph of a cabin on a cliff in the Catskills, a scene that, in its combination of sunlight and mist, seemed to suggest the possibility of reconciling oppositional forces. After ushering us in and settling us on the couch, he eased himself into a low armchair, his answering machine and a box of Kleenex for weepy patients within easy reach on the floor, balanced a legal pad on his thigh, and spelled out the benefits of mediation.

First of all, he said, it avoided the financial ruination that adversarial divorces often produced; he had known divorce lawyers who had sued their own clients to force them, in order to pay their legal bills, to sell the house the lawyer had won for them during the divorce proceeding. But a mediated settlement offered a benefit even more valuable than saving money, Yahm continued. It allowed the husband and wife to maintain an amicable relationship. That was crucial for their own states of mind; he had seen people reduced to embittered, vengeful, hate-filled husks, not so much by the decision to split up as by the antagonistic emotions a litigated divorce provoked. It was even more important for the mental health of their children. The key to mediation, he went on, was compromise. Both parties had to be willing to accept less, maybe a little less and maybe even substantially less, than what they felt they deserved. Without mutual concessions, he said, mediation would fail.

Maureen and I looked at each other and nodded. We had already agreed that we would share joint custody of our daughter but that she would live with Maureen. Yahm asked us a series of boilerplate questions about visitation schedules, birthdays, holidays, religious divorces, the eventualities of relocation. Rapidly nodding in encouragement as he scribbled notes on his legal pad, he was focused, patient, creative, and thorough. I liked him. We sailed through all of the preliminary matters and then came to the only real issue that existed: money.

My wife and I both wanted, for Jessica's sake at least, to maintain an amicable relationship, and we were determined not to allow squabbling over finances to ruin that. Neither Maureen nor I was greedy or vindictive. And in any event, since I wasn't in risk arbitrage or corporate finance, there simply wasn't that much money. I had a couple of meager IRA's and a Mexican mutual fund that had lost half its value since the peso collapsed. I also had my salary—decent enough—although the business I was in was looking increasingly obsolete and precarious. Our possessions consisted of Cooch, the long-haired cat that we bought for Jessica when she was four, a used car, a cheap stereo, two faded yellow sofas whose upholstery Cooch had shredded, four thin Persian carpets also ravaged by the cat's claws, some nineteenth-century botanical prints, several hundred books with sun-bleached spines, and a small, overpriced house near the beach we'd acquired in a last-ditch effort to keep together the disintegrating marriage and had ended up renting out at a loss. What was there to haggle about?

I said I was prepared to support my wife. Since she hadn't worked in several years and might have difficulty finding a job, I told Yahm, I would pay her "maintenance" for seven years, until Jessica turned eighteen and left for college. I thought I was being eminently reasonable. Seven years was plenty of time, I figured, for Maureen to retrain, to go back to school, to do whatever it took to update herself and prepare for the workplace of the twenty-first century. Maureen nodded in agreement and Yahm wrote it down on his legal pad.

At the next session we took up the question of expenses. I thought the discussion should begin with what was available to be spent. I told Yahm how much I could afford to give Maureen based on what I made. Supporting two households on my paycheck would require substantial sacrifices by both of us.

Maureen, however, had brought with her a list of what she thought were her reasonable expenses, including not just rent, utilities, and food, but entertainment, travel, and the wages of Dorothy, the elderly black woman who cleaned the apartment every other week. She thought I should provide her with enough money to continue this unextravagant but comfortable life and survive on whatever was left over.

"I can't live off that!" I said.

"Well, earn more money," she replied. We were sitting side by side on Yahm's couch, each with our own legal pad on which we'd made our own financial tabulations.

"How?"

"Freelance. Write a book. You'll find something."

I turned to Yahm. His eyebrows were raised in anticipation.

"Is that a possibility?" he asked.

I didn't want to earn more money simply to support someone who wasn't working and who, I felt, could find a job if she had to. If anything, I felt like earning *less* money. I could feel the first small tug of the antagonism that if left unchecked would lead to war. The temptation to yield to it was strong.

"I'm supposed to earn *more* money?" I asked in return. "What's my incentive?"

"Meeting your responsibilities," Yahm said.

The meeting left me feeling throttled and desperate. I was afraid I was going to be forced to take on an appalling financial burden from which I myself would receive no enjoyment or benefit. Did my "responsibilities" now truly require slavish self-sacrifice? Was I supposed to exhaust myself earning substantial amounts of money only to live in semipoverty while turning most of my income over to a wife who disliked me and who said she was unable to work because rush-hour subways made her anxious and, anyway, she needed to be at home when our daughter returned from school? There had to be some alternative.

That afternoon, instead of returning to the office, I went to a bookstore and, as furtively as if I were looking for pornography, asked the clerk where I could find the books on divorce. She was cheerful and helpful and pretended not to notice my embarrassment. They were in the Self-Help section, she said, between Relationships and Addiction & Recovery. The niche seemed appropriate.

I was looking for some sort of legal guide, but I became distracted by the volumes offering solace and insight into the emotional condition of the divorced. The first book I picked up was *Crazy Time*. It had a chapter about people who, once their marriages ended, turned into Passion Addicts. "You're at risk of becoming a Passion Repeater," the author warned, "and being stuck at the Hummingbird level of love, which is another form of Divorce Flameout." The inanity of the language amazed me. I put down *Crazy Time* and flipped through a crimson paperback with the title *Divorce Hangover*. "Send yourself flowers," the author urged. "Don't analyze whether or not you deserve them. You *need* them!" There was a book called *Between Love & Hate*. "Find an outlet to release strong emotions safely," the author recommended. "For example, sports, exercise, throwing darts at a photo of your spouse, tearing a picture of your spouse into shreds, attaching a photo of him or her to the bottom of your shoe and stomping around for ten minutes a day."

Did people, I wondered, really take comfort from such bilge? A depressing thought. I picked up *Get Rid of Him*. This book was blatantly prodivorce; its table of contents included the chapters "Get Rid of Him If You're on the Begging End," "Get Rid of Him If He's Jealous of You or Does Not Empower You," "Get Rid of Him If You Can't Stand to Go to Bed with Him," "Get Rid of

Him If You're Staying Only for the Money, the Security, or the Children," and "Get Rid of Him If He's Chronically Unemployed." But most of the books opposed divorce. There was clearly more money to be made in that message, and it was, I supposed, a message of hope. I looked at a book called *Divorce Busters.* "I don't believe in 'saving marriages,'" wrote the author. "I believe in divorcing marriages and beginning a new one—with the same partner." But as a book called *The Case against Divorce* demonstrated, the message that divorce should be avoided was also a message of fear. "Discover the lures, the lies, and the emotional traps of divorce," the book's jacket promised, "plus the seven vital reasons to stay together." Skimming its unilluminating sections ("Three Lies about Being Single That Destroy Marriage"; "The Crime of 'Mid-Life Crisis'"; "Divorce Won't Solve Your Problems"), I was surprised to read that the author herself was divorced and happily remarried. She had actually dedicated her book to her second husband—"Michael, who reminds me daily of the value of marriage"—but warned her readers that they should regard her as an exception. Most men and women, she said, could not count on the good fortune she had enjoyed.

I turned away from this slag heap of alliteration, cliché, and dishonesty to a volume with a refreshingly neutral title, *The Divorce Book.* It contained a chapter, "The Fundamental Flaw of Mediation," which beckoned with ominous insistence. "Unfortunately, mediation doesn't work as smoothly in actuality as in theory," the author, a matrimonial lawyer, wrote. "I know because husbands and wives enlist my services when they fail to reach agreement through mediation, after they've accepted a mediated agreement and realized they've struck a terrible deal, sometimes even secretly in the middle of mediation to protect themselves against agreeing to anything they'll regret later." The words chilled me. I was on the verge of agreeing to financial obligations that could burden me for years—*years!*—without any serious independent review of my position. I decided then that at the very least I should discuss my situation with Rhenquist.

Dick Rhenquist was a stock and insurance broker who had sold me a disability policy ten years earlier and invited me back to his office once a year to discuss my finances. He was waiting for the day when I would make enough money to become a viable invest-ment client. That day hadn't yet arrived, but he was certainly pros-pering from other clients, for he had moved every two or three years into a more lavish suite of offices, and when I went to see him, two weeks after that moment of self-protective clarification in the bookstore, he had moved yet again and now worked out of a large paneled room, with a view of the Hudson, in the upper reaches of a neo-Gothic skyscraper.

Rhenquist sat me down in the leather wing chair across from his carved partner's desk, the choppy river and the rising Newark skyline visible behind him, and summoned his secretary to bring me a cup of coffee. Rhenquist's pale face and lank hair and dark, shapeless suits always seemed vaguely funereal, but there was nothing grim about his personality. He had the powerful grip, the unflagging optimism, and reactionary politics of a Marine colonel, and his response to my account of my impending separation trig-gered his Darwinian instincts. He became unabashedly martial.

"This is war," he said.

"Not with us. I hope."

"You know what's the object in a divorce?"

"What?"

"To avoid getting screwed. You know what's the only way to avoid getting screwed?"

"No."

"You screw her first. Preemptive retaliation. Here's what I

want you to do. Clean out your bank account before she does it for you. Hide your assets, your valuable personal effects, your tax statements, your canceled checks, diaries, credit-card receipts, anything potentially damaging or anything she can use to establish a level of consumption that will justify a level of alimony. Get them out of your house before she photocopies them, because she will, surreptitiously if she has to. Her lawyer will tell her to do it if she's got a good one."

"We're seeing a mediator," I said.

"Well, she's a fool if she doesn't hire a lawyer. She's probably got one now. The mediation is probably a ruse to buy time until she can put together a complete financial picture. You haven't moved out, have you?"

"Not yet, but I'm looking for a place."

"Don't go. If you leave, she can argue abandonment, which gives her a claim to the apartment and all the possessions and to custody of your daughter."

"She wouldn't do that."

"You think. Wait till she starts following the advice of her lawyer. You don't want to leave the house. What you want to do, if anything, is drive her out. That will strengthen your position."

Rhenquist's secretary brought me my coffee in a china cup on a tray. It was one of those flavored blends—almond vanilla, Irish creme—that for a reason I couldn't fathom had come to betoken class.

"It's not that kind of a separation, Dick," I said. "It's not adversarial."

"It's always adversarial. Maybe not in the beginning, but by the end it's always adversarial."

I shook my head.

"Make a list of your wife's vulnerabilities," Rhenquist went on. "Prepare to barter custody for alimony. Sell everything to one of your sisters for a dollar and then buy it back when this is all over. And if Maureen really tries to come after you, you move to Belize and become a citizen there. She won't be able to get a dime."

"Belize?"

"There are no extradition treaties of any sort. I've had a couple of clients who've done it."

"I can't move to Belize."

"You can. I'm not saying you should. I'm not saying you're going to. But you can. It's a comforting thing to know. You're not necessarily trapped. You have an escape route. You don't have to become one of these guys who's stripped naked, who has everything, and I mean *everything,* taken by some man-hating judge in family court. And it happens, buddy. I've seen it happen."

I remembered the man whose daughter played softball with my daughter, the one I ran into on the subway whose wife had gotten custody, child support, and maintenance. The man labored daily for wages he never touched himself to provide for a woman who despised him and a daughter he saw only at softball games. And suddenly, I *could* see myself moving to Belize. Tropical beaches, rain forest, a scandalously low cost of living—with a fax machine and a laptop, I could probably carve out a comfortable existence.

"Belize," I said.

Rhenquist looked at me across his desk. "Keep it in the back of your mind."

The "Belize option," as I began to think of it, was of course far-fetched, but it comforted me nonetheless. Over the next couple of sessions with Howard Yahm, my wife and I worked out a financial compromise. I would give her a monthly check that was more than I had been prepared to pay but less than the amount needed to cover her complete list of theoretical expenses. The sum included child support and maintenance and would last until my daughter turned eighteen. In addition to that money I would pay my daughter's school tuition and, when the time came, her college tuition.

The vastness of the sums to which I was committing myself left me light-headed. Every last dollar I made was accounted for. I would be able to save nothing. There would be no extravagances. And any untoward change in my professional fortunes would quickly bankrupt me.

"It's so much money," I complained to Yahm. "What if I lose my job?"

He shrugged. "You'll get another. Look at it this way. It's not forever. By the time you're fifty you'll be a free man."

That was hardly a consoling thought. It meant the span of my life, before the onset of old age, had been reduced to a decade of penury and servitude followed by a decade of freedom.

The following week Yahm drew up a draft version of our agreement, gave us each a copy, and suggested we show it to a lawyer. I didn't see the point in this. We had gone to Yahm in order to avoid involving lawyers. What would a lawyer say, when showed the contract, except that he could secure me or my wife a better deal?

Maureen did retain a lawyer. "It's for my own protection," she said. And, I learned in early November, he had recommended some changes.

"What changes?" I asked. I was in my office—I tried to spend as little time as possible at home those days—and we were talking on the phone. Maureen refused to describe her lawyer's recommendations.

"We'll have to discuss them with Yahm," she said.

The following afternoon we met again at the mediator's office. Maureen, wearing a gray silk shawl, looked tired but determined. She had her legal pad out and was playing with her reading glasses. Her lawyer, she explained, thought I should pay her maintenance for the rest of her life. *Lifetime maintenance!* I hadn't even known the concept was still in use until a few months earlier, when my friend Adam, the one who had moved into his office after leaving his wife, told me that his lawyer had advised him he should be prepared to support her for the rest of her life. She was fifty, the lawyer had said, and hadn't worked in more than ten years. One of the many feminist judges in family court could easily rule that since she had given up her career for her husband, he was obliged to support her. Adam might have to carry his wife, who had always seemed to me quite capable of working, for the rest of his life. The idea was galling. It ran contrary to the principles of independence I thought were at the core of feminism. And now, a few months later, my own wife, who was still in her forties, was demanding lifetime maintenance herself.

"You want me," I asked, "to support you for the rest of your life?"

"Well," my wife said. "We've been married for twelve years. I'm entitled to it."

I'm entitled to it. That wasn't the sort of phrase Maureen normally used. I could see her lawyer advising her to ask for lifetime maintenance, could see her hesitate at the sheer enormity of the proposition, and then see the lawyer lean across his desk, fix her with a level gaze, and say, "You're entitled to it." And in no time she had convinced herself she was.

While Yahm stroked his beard and listened, Maureen insisted she needed the maintenance because she couldn't get a job. She had supported herself before we got married, she said, and had only stopped working when Jessica was born. I said she hadn't stopped working at my behest. Plenty of women we knew had had children and gone back to work. I would have been happy if, once Jessica was in school full-time, she had done the same thing.

This argument brought us back to the core dispute in our marriage: the lack of respect we each believed our contributions to it had received. Maureen felt that she had given up her career—fitful though it was—to raise her daughter and that I failed to appreciate both her sacrifice and the hard work child-rearing entailed. Maureen was right. Because I didn't consider it a sacrifice. I thought she could have gone back to work if she had wanted to.

Maureen pointed out that she had gone back to work, if only part-time, at *Town & Country,* and after being laid off had been unable to find work elsewhere. And anyway, she said, she was needed at home.

"Who would have looked after Jessica when she came home from school?" Maureen asked. "I didn't want her coming home to an empty house. I didn't want to trust her to some strange nanny who might not show up."

I thought arrangements could have been made. Other people managed to make them. I thought a job would have been good for her, that it would have stimulated her, and eased her chronic dissatisfaction.

"My job has been raising Jessica," Maureen said. "And if you look at her you'll see I've done a pretty good job. She's a pretty special kid."

"You're right," I said. And she *was* right. Still, I felt, if she chose to stay home she should recognize that for what it was—a choice, one she had freely, willingly made. And I also felt that if that was her choice she should consider herself fortunate, even privileged, not deprived, to be able to make it, that she should feel grateful rather than resentful. Now, to Yahm, she was presenting her choice not to work as evidence of a sacrifice that had robbed her of a career and required that I support her for the rest of her life.

We think we understand things from reading or hearing about them, but we never really do until we experience them, and until that moment I had not fully grasped the way in which marriage is a *binding* legal contract. It takes your fate, your *life,* out of your own hands and turns it over to the appointed guardians of society, to lawyers and judges who have the authority to dictate to you the terms of your own existence. The thought flooded me with panic. Previously, the need to keep the fragile marriage and then the tentatively cooperative separation working had exercised a restraining force on me. Now, with the demand for lifetime maintenance hanging in the air like some grotesquely unjust prison sentence, I wasn't interested in cooperation, and I began to shout at Maureen.

Maureen, undaunted, shouted back. Yahm let the storm play itself out for a few moments before raising his own voice to silence us. To me, he pointed out that Maureen could probably find a doctor who would say that in his opinion her medical condition rendered her incapable of working and a judge who would accept it. He suggested shuffling some of my negligible assets back to me to make the concession more amenable.

"But—*lifetime* maintenance?" I asked.

Yahm held out his hands, palms up in a gesture of resignation, and shrugged his shoulders. I could tell he had been here many times before. He had watched other clients sink back into their chairs, staggered by the monstrous weight of the obligation that until then they were unaware they had assumed in getting married. I looked at Maureen. She was studying her hands. I thought fleetingly of the Belize option. I heard myself exhale. I agreed to lifetime maintenance.

Outside afterward, standing on the sidewalk in the harsh November sun, my wife and I both felt relieved. The knowledge that I wouldn't leave her to fend for herself in a hostile world reassured her. I could take some satisfaction in shouldering my responsibilities. The cruel words we had spoken were, if not forgotten, dismissed.

"So when you get the contract, you'll sign it and send it on to me?" I asked.

She nodded. She was fastening the toggle buttons on her winter coat, a benchwarmer with a honey-yellow canvas shell. It was always easy to spot her in that coat; I think I liked it more than she did.

We kissed—I felt a grudging respect for her for standing up for what she wanted—and went our separate ways.

Chapter 30

In mid-December, after two months of searching sporadically and half-heartedly for an apartment, I was lured into a real estate office by a set of ads, hand-printed in Magic Marker and tacked to a sidewalk signboard, promising miraculous deals. The office, down a narrow flight of stairs from the street, was occupied by a man with psoriasis and a muffler around his neck who was talking on the telephone and didn't bother to look up when I entered. A woman sat at a small metal desk wedged behind the door. She was elderly, shriveled and hunched, with a shank of gray hair hanging over one eye as she scribbled on a page of figures.

The office had such an indisputably hard-luck atmosphere I would not have been surprised if the elderly woman had been wearing gloves with the fingers cut off. All they'll have, I thought, is short-term sublets and cheap renovations in ugly neighborhoods, rejects that the Montague Street agencies wouldn't trouble to list.

I was about to leave when the woman looked up and pointed at the metal folding chair beside her desk. While I was sure the ads on the signboard outside were false or at the very least misleading, I couldn't resist their promise. I asked the woman about them. She brushed her hand in the air, sweeping them aside as if unworthy of discussion, and insisted that before we discussed available apartments I fill out a lengthy form (price range, priorities, income, bank balance, job history, personal references). When I finished, she read it, mumbling to herself, then told me she had just what I was looking for and would show it to me right now if I had a car. I said I did, parked a few blocks away.

"Can you bring it around?" she asked. "I don't like to walk far when it's icy out."

We drove down a commercial thoroughfare into an old Italian neighborhood already decorated for Christmas. A cold December wind buffeted the oversized Styrofoam snowflakes and the plastic candy canes strung on wires between streetlights and ruffled the green synthetic fir on the imitation evergreen boughs twisted snakelike around the posts. Among the Laundromats and butcher shops and dingy video-rental stores that lined the street were mysterious social clubs whose windows had been ostentatiously blacked out.

"Mafia," the real estate agent whispered with conspiratorial pride. Making it clear that she considered the presence of the criminal organization a selling point, she added, "They keep the neighborhood safe."

The apartment was in a converted chocolate factory. Its immediate surroundings lacked charm. The Christmas ornaments on the streetlights seemed even skimpier and scruffier than those up the avenue. An elevated section of the subway flanked one side of the building, and an elevated expressway another. The roar was continuous—the sound of surf on a windy day. The air was flecked with soot and seemed to tremble. Beyond the building, across a busy avenue, was a sprawling public housing complex built in the fifties and now in an advanced state of deterioration. The social clubs, I realized, probably were a selling point.

But the parking was easier here than in our neighborhood; I found a spot, to the real estate agent's relief, directly in front of the main door. And the apartment she showed me, looking onto a spacious courtyard covered with grass and lined with now leafless poplars, was actually quieter than our house. It had two bedrooms, freshly varnished pine floors, high ceilings, an airy living room blessed with a set of broad industrial windows facing into the white wintry sun, and even, in a jaunty architectural touch, a freestanding support column topped by a simple plaster crown. It was light, quiet, within my modest budget. And to cap it all off, the real estate agent said, since the market was slow, the owner would pay half her fee. That seemed a portent in itself.

The agent studied me, a sly, avaricious glint in her eye, and said, "You're a lucky man."

I nodded. That was how I had always thought of myself. There was, I saw, no reason not to take the apartment, which meant, suddenly, I had lost my excuse for delaying the move.

Three weeks later, on a wintry afternoon, my wife and I called our daughter into our bedroom. She could tell by our expressions, the willed composure, that what was about to transpire carried a tragic gravity, a frightening emotional bottomlessness unlike anything she had ever experienced. We were leading her, she instinctively knew, out into water that was over her head.

Our bedroom never had good light. It faced north, into the branches of a locust tree, and on that late afternoon—a Friday, chosen so my daughter could have the weekend to adjust to the new situation—snow clouds obscured the sun, and the room was steeped in shadow. The gloom eased things. It dulled the edge. My wife and I had both been struggling with a palpable horror of this moment, dreading it the way you would dread a scheduled amputation. Bright light would have made it unbearable.

Sitting on our bed, our daughter between us, we started to proceed through the inevitable, overrehearsed, and overrationalized points: we argued too much; these arguments created tension; we would all be happier; it was no one's fault, certainly not our daughter's. She nodded at first. Tears welled into her eyes but she was absorbing the information, and then she blurted out in a tone of piercing fearfulness, "You're not getting divorced, are you?"

It was not the mere fact of my physical departure that disturbed her the most. It was the prospect of irrevocability. She wanted to know: Was the small world she inhabited, the one that at that minute was collapsing around her, ever to be restored?

My wife was crying, my daughter was crying, we were all crying, mourners grieving at the death of the family we had been. "Everything's going to be all right," I said. "We'll all be a lot happier. Everything will be all right."

I looked at my wife. She nodded. And then, my daughter nodded too. She couldn't quite comprehend how that might come about, how everything would work out for the best and we'd all be happier, but despite what we had just inflicted on her, her trust in our ability to protect her remained so ingrained, so instinctive, that she seemed to believe us.

At the same time we both felt strangely, even perversely, relieved, to have this particular hurdle behind us, and to be able, after so many years of holding back our feelings, to finally air them. The catharsis left us almost giddy. We took my daughter over to see my new apartment. It was only ten minutes away. She brought stuffed animals to put on what was to be *her* bed. And then we all went out to dinner, to our favorite restaurant, to celebrate.

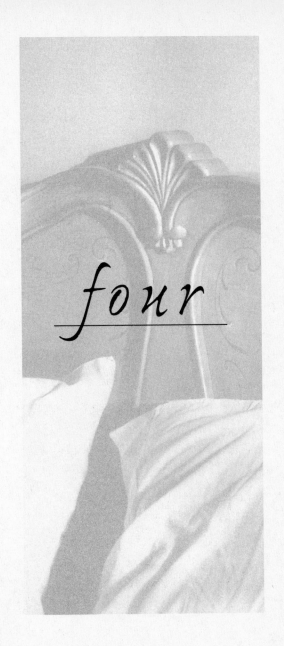

four

Chapter 31

The months that followed were not easy. I saw my apartment as transitional, a place where I was marking time until my new life took shape, and so I had hung nothing on its huge white walls. Waking up those first winter months in its silent emptiness, its arctic void, in the white bed in the white bedroom lit by diffuse white light, could fill me with a loneliness so intense and bleak that it was frightening.

I became as easily startled as a child. The pigeon flapping at the window, the tap on the shoulder, the telephone's ring—they all rattled me. Free time was frightening. To fill it, I played tennis and racquetball three or four times a week, and worked out at the gym on the nights I had nothing to do. I did this as much for the camaraderie as for the exercise. I wanted to hear the sound of other people's voices even if they weren't talking to me. I watched basketball on television, which I had never done before. It made me feel connected to something larger, even if only the fortunes of a handful of rich athletes and the other people rooting for them, and after half a season I had worked up a pale version of the true fan's vicarious engagement. Silence frightened me as well. I turned on the radio as soon as I awoke, listened to talk shows, which provided a similar illusory but comforting connectedness. I kept the radio on until I left the apartment and turned it back on as soon as I returned.

While I had read the studies about how men's income rose after divorce, I had also seen the statistics that showed divorced men were much more likely to commit suicide than divorced women. And suicide did begin to seem rational. I was not consumed with plans to kill myself, but from time to time it appeared to me, in the abstract, as an alternative worth considering. I could understand it. I could see how easy, how natural, even how irresistible such plans could be to someone who found that, without quite knowing when or why, he had drifted into an endless fog.

What I felt was not regret but bewilderment and despair, and it made me, when I was around others, even more brittle and snappish than before. I was no longer working as a political columnist by then. It had been interesting for a while, but in the end I found out I was less drawn to politicians and their policies—subjects in any event exhaustively covered by other journalists—than to stories no one else had written about, true tales (to use a phrase one of my editors liked to throw around), about ordinary people in extraordinary situations. I wrote about a woman whose false memories of sexual abuse, implanted by a therapist, had destroyed her family; about a young man sentenced to life in prison for a rape he didn't commit; about transsexuals and their opposites, men who had surgical penis enlargement in the hope that this would magically enhance their self-confidence. What attracted me at the time, I realized later, were encounters with people who had undergone some sort of violent transformation.

I worried constantly about my wife. I was afraid that Maureen, in her determination to get me out of her life, had not been thinking clearly about what that life would be like once I had gone. Had she really thought through the difficulties she would face raising our daughter on her own? About the financial constraints she would be under? About how she would cope if her illness progressed and her symptoms worsened? Preoccupied with how unhappy I had been making her, she had refused to concern herself with any of these things. But I did. And I sometimes thought that even if she wanted me to leave, even if it was against her will, I ought to have stayed for her sake.

The state of our old apartment seemed to confirm my suspicions. After I left, it seemed to have fallen into disarray. Whenever I returned—to drop off my daughter and pick up my mail, to take down the storm windows or replace an overhead lightbulb in the kitchen or clean my daughter's aquarium, performing the husbandly duties my wife still expected of me—I noticed signs of increasing disorder and scruffiness. The cat had utterly destroyed the sun-faded upholstery on both arms of both sofas. Knots of its hair nestled in the corners of the rooms and floated along the floorboards. Unread junk mail lay in piles on the piano and dining table and cupboard. Dust coated the tops of the books. Recipes torn from newspapers and affixed to the refrigerator door with magnets curled and yellowed. The wicker chair near the rear window, the one with the direct sunlight and the Boston fern, where I used to like to read on weekend mornings, was unraveling. A plastic bag full of old bottles of suntan lotion had hung from the handle of the living-room door for more than a year.

The place is coming apart, I thought, and my wife is oblivious to it. She needs me, I thought, she can't make it without me.

But then I thought, maybe the apartment has always been in this condition, and I've only begun to notice it because I no longer live here. Maybe I was exaggerating or even imagining the disarray in order to feel needed. Maybe, I thought, she doesn't really need me at all.

———————

Throughout that time, Maureen and I were both practically sick with worry over the effect of our separation on Jessica. A book published a few years earlier, *Second Chances: Men, Women and Children a Decade After Divorce,* purported to show how the children of divorced parents grow up to become depressed, insecure, ambivalent adults. Even children who seemed to adjust to divorce could, years later, suddenly find their anxieties erupting in a delayed reaction the writers called a Sleeper Effect. After I moved out, I read *Second Chances,* which was a mistake. The book incensed me. I took it as a personal rebuke. Its conclusions seemed so transparently fraudulent, so stupidly unscientific. The writers used no control group. They had compared the children of divorce neither with the children of happily married couples nor with those of unhappily married couples. While the book was treated in the popular press as a blanket condemnation of divorce, in many of the case studies the authors described it was not the divorce itself but the antagonistic manner in which the divorce was handled, or the tensions that came from living with parents who couldn't stand each other, that caused the depression, insecurity, and ambivalence among the children involved. And anyway, I thought at the time, what adult these days, no matter how happy his childhood may have been, doesn't go through periods of depression? Who doesn't experience insecurity and ambivalence?

Nonetheless, *Second Chances* had been greeted with the kind of acclaim that invariably accompanies a book whose appearance validates a new set of cultural convictions. My wife and I were operating in the shadow of its supposedly scientific conclusions, and so, when Maureen decided Jessica ought to see a therapist, I reluctantly consented. Who knew what kind of "repressed memories" the therapist might implant? But Jessica thought the sessions were pointless. She resented the therapist's probing, and after a few months the treatment, such as it was, petered out.

When we tried to talk to our daughter about how she felt, she insisted everything was fine. At first, her most pressing concern seemed social: she was humiliated when one girl told the rest of her class that my wife and I had split up. But I began to notice she had a quiet, stricken look on those evenings I picked her up to spend the night at my place. Finally, I asked what was wrong.

"I don't like sleeping over. I never have all my stuff. My friends never know where to call me."

My heart froze. I launched into the standard blather about how lucky she was to have two houses.

"I don't *want* two houses," she said in a jagged voice. "I want one house."

Moments like this made me wonder whether the decision to leave had been a dreadful mistake. I had thought I was acting with moral clarity, that I had in the end, unexpectedly and unintentionally, achieved a sort of moral self-definition: I was doing not what I wanted to do but what was right for everyone. But maybe, moments like this made me think, what I had been engaged in was an elaborate ruse, an act of self-justification. Had the breakdown become irrevocable only because I wanted it to be? Had I in fact willed it that way?

But all of us have to learn to live with uncertainty. Uncertainty itself, in fact, indicates the authenticity of the enterprise. Only the absolutists, blindly adhering to their codes of duty, and the narcissists, who lack any sense of obligation altogether, are free from doubt. The rest of us, struggling for moral coherence in a world that no longer imposes it, are not so lucky.

Maureen and I counted on each other to get through these moments; she had more than her share. Separating, it surprised us to discover as the months went by, left us freer to express ourselves than we had been before. We were no longer paralyzed by the need to preserve the artificial peace. Less afraid that the doubts and insecurities we revealed would be used against us, we became more open about them. We respected each other's frailties. Separating seemed to bring out the best in both of us.

Chapter 32

A lex called me the following summer. We hadn't seen each other in three years, and I suggested we get together. We met for lunch in the same restaurant, and sat again at one of the tiny tables under the same sepia photographs of Venice. She seemed tired and preoccupied, but she was still beautiful. She ordered a vodka and tonic.

She had married the executive recruiter, she said, and had moved into his spacious, impersonally furnished apartment. They lived the overscheduled lives of people in their orbit. Alex described for me her typical day: a predawn workout followed by a breakfast presentation; a morning of meetings, a client lunch, an afternoon of sales pitches; business cocktails and business dinners three nights a week; an appointment calendar booked two months in advance. It was a glamorous and eventful but also grinding and claustrophobic existence; she and her husband both faced a remorseless pressure to meet and then exceed their projected earnings. To escape on weekends, they bought a farmhouse in Litchfield County and, to reach it, a hulking Mitsubishi Montero. But the country solitude bored her husband, and he spent much of his time there on the telephone. At his insistence they postponed and then canceled the plans to have a child. He already had three children; his eldest daughter was two years younger than Alex.

As time passed, Alex said, her husband began to weary of her independence and assertiveness. Her constant inquiries about what he was thinking, and why, and what he was feeling, and why, grated on him. He was too old, he realized, too set in his ways, for the fierce intimacy she demanded. She questioned his decisions, and the need he had to prevail in their disputes tired him. He had come to feel intimidated by Alex's sexual appetites—the raw desire that he had at first found to be such a source of regeneration. He felt inadequate to it, which made him despise himself. He blamed her for that also, and their sex life dwindled. Feeling besieged, he retreated inside himself.

As he withdrew she realized that her dream of what marriage entailed—companionship, emotional truth, children—was in jeopardy, and she pursued him more avidly than ever. The more she questioned, the harder she tried to draw him out, the more recalcitrant he became. She took him of course to see her therapist, Sharon—I was surprised and then not so surprised that after all these years she was still in treatment with Sharon; it was her most enduring relationship—and while he agreed to go to the office with the Mondrian print and the small window looking out onto the sidewalk, his failure to cooperate once he got there was childlike in its hostility. On those nights when they were both home he acted as if he had lost the faculty of speech.

"We didn't make love enough, and you know how important sex is to me," she said. "But I figured I could live with that. What I couldn't stand was the silence. On the way out to the country he would just sit there staring at the road. This was our time together. We were supposed to talk. I would ask him, 'What are you thinking?' and he would say, 'Nothing.' It would drive me insane. I would say, 'You must be thinking something. *Tell* me. *Talk* to me.' And then he would say something like, 'I was thinking about how in another two hundred miles the odometer will change to fifty thousand, and all the nines will turn into zeroes.' I couldn't decide which was worse, that I was married to someone who wouldn't tell me what he was thinking unless I pulled it out of him or that his thoughts were so boring."

They had agreed to split up, Alex said. She was on her second vodka and tonic. She raised the glass and said, "I'm never getting married again."

My own feelings on this matter were far less clear. In fact, my failed marriage had done little to diminish my faith in the institution itself. I still believed a good marriage could be, or should be, possible. This conviction was instinctive and probably sentimental. It certainly ran contrary to the rapidly accumulating body of evidence. Alex's failed second marriage was just one example. Every single one of the women in the play group my wife had joined after our daughter was born had gotten divorced. Every single one. That summer Sheryl, the woman I was still seeing, left her husband. He never saw it coming and, when she announced she was going, never pressed her for a reason, contenting himself with the delusion that her behavior was the result of an emotional crisis caused by the death of her father a year earlier. Around the same time, Sheryl's brother was abandoned by his wife, who moved with their daughter to New Haven to live with a woman she had met on the Internet. Four months later, Sheryl's mother-in-law, who was in her sixties, left her second husband, packing her things and moving out one weekend while he was obliviously enjoying himself at their country house; on his return, her lawyer—she was the one with the money—presented him with a formal statement.

I found it almost impossible to believe that someone who had been married for ten or fifteen years could one day simply walk out on a husband or wife and never look back. Did such people live entirely in the present, deaf to the music of their own histories? Or had their marriages been so flat, so toneless, that once ended and consigned to the past they produced no reverberations? For my wife and me, it was very different. Our marriage kept calling to us.

"We've got to sign the agreement," Maureen said. She had telephoned me at my new office, a small gray room with a single window overlooking an empty lot and the tar-paper roof of a nineteenth-century tenement that now housed a Chinese restaurant. It was a mild September day. Three cooks in dirty white uniforms stood on the roof, smoking cigarettes and kick-boxing. The rituals of vice, the rituals of violence, the rituals of disengagement. Who said modern life lacked ritual?

"I've been asking you to sign it for more than a year," I said.

It was exactly eleven months since our last meeting with Yahm, the meeting at which I had agreed to lifetime maintenance. Since then I had encouraged her to sign the agreement he had drafted, but she became so evasive whenever I brought it up that I had finally stopped asking. I knew the reason for her hesitation; she was afraid she wouldn't be able to take care of herself, and as long as we remained legally married, she felt protected. The truth was, I had begun to think that I might be better off if I didn't sign it. Why lock myself into a commitment to pay her a fixed level of maintenance for the rest of her life?

"I've been afraid," she said. "But we've got to sign it."

"What's made you change your mind?"

"I'm afraid we'll become like the Webers."

The Webers were engaged in a battle that genuinely horrified both of us. Adam Weber was tall, handsome, and shy, and so afraid of Claire, his domineering and overwrought and, as she aged, increasingly hysterical wife, that he had left her without warning, and for that she could never forgive him. Now, at the mere sound of each other's voice, rage choked them both, so they communicated only by fax.

Nathan, the Webers' son, lived with Claire during the week and spent alternate weekends with his father. I had seen Adam the day before Maureen called, and he had described the latest trouble, which had started the previous Friday, when Claire arrived to pick up Nathan after school and discovered Adam there as well. Both parents thought it was *their* weekend with the boy. Claire allowed Adam to take Nathan, but during the week she persuaded her son that Adam's behavior was outrageous. Nathan sent his father a fax informing him that it had been "inappropriate" for Adam to pick him up at the school that Friday. Consequently, Nathan said, he didn't want Adam to attend his upcoming performance at school in *The Wind in the Willows*.

Adam was devastated. He sent Nathan a fax calling his behavior unacceptable and demanding an apology. Several days passed in which Nathan failed to respond, and Adam finally called Claire. She admitted she had received the fax but had not given it to Nathan, she said, because she thought it might upset him.

Adam was driven frantic by the idea that his wife could, and would, prevent him from speaking to his son. He had called his son's school for advice about attending the performance and the headmaster had forbidden him to come. The headmaster said that if there should be a fight after the performance over who should take the child home, the school would have to call the police and turn him over to them while the parents summoned their lawyers and argued the custody question before a judge.

"It scares me," my wife said. "We can't let something like that happen to us."

I agreed. It scared me too, and it sickened me. I saw how easy it was to surrender to suspicion, bitterness, and hatred, to lose sight of what was best for ourselves and our children. Once you've become convinced that the husband or wife who has left you is really evil, you don't think you are poisoning your child's mind when you warn him about his other parent. You are alerting him to evident danger.

"It won't happen to us," I said.

"We have to remain friends, at all costs. We have to."

"I know."

"Do you promise me we will?"

"I promise."

"And we have to sign the agreement. So we won't have mis-understandings like they did."

For the past year, fear had prevented her from signing. Now a greater fear impelled her to take the step she had been dreading. Is that what all our lives actually consist of? I wondered. While we believe we are moving forward, toward our objectives, are we in fact only in flight from a series of perceived perils?

I had left almost all of my belongings back at the brownstone. Not just what was technically joint property but things on which I either had a greater emotional claim, such as the Chinese chest my parents had given us as a wedding present, or actually, indisputably, owned. There was a bow and a quiverful of handmade arrows I'd acquired by bartering with a bushman on my trip to Botswana. Framed black-and-white photographs, atop the living room bookcase, of my parents as children and my grandparents as young adults, of my great-grandmother and her sisters looking stern in high-collared blouses. Some art books I'd received as gifts.

While I was sure Maureen would never even notice if any of these were missing, I didn't want to tell her I was taking them and possibly provoke an argument over stripping the house. One day, when I came by to pick up Jessica, Maureen was out, and it occurred to me to inconspicuously remove two books on Van Dyck and the Rizzoli series on New York architecture that I had always prized. Jessica, I was surprised to find, noticed and was troubled by what I was doing.

"Where are you taking those?" she asked. She was on the verge of adolescence, tall and lanky. She dressed in bell-bottom jeans and dirty running shoes, wore her backpack everywhere, and was capable, from time to time, of startlingly mature perceptions.

"Over to my place," I said. The answer didn't satisfy her. "They're mine," I added.

She pointed to one of the books on Van Dyck. "That's one of Mommy's favorites," she said.

I knew this was untrue. I doubted if Maureen had ever even read it. "Well, it was a Christmas gift to me from your grandparents."

Which *was* true. But beside the point. I put the books in my car, having utterly failed to see from my daughter's perspective what it was that I was doing. Worse, a few weeks later, under similar circumstances, I decided to retrieve a few of the framed family photographs.

"Why are you taking them?" Jessica asked, again troubled.

"I don't know. They're mine, I guess."

"But"——she pointed to the photograph of my mother as an eight-year-old girl—"I always liked that." Then she pointed to the photograph of my father at the age of six. "That one too."

It was only then that I realized how mistaken I'd been in assuming that all of these things were mine just because they had once belonged to me. They were part of the house in which my daughter had grown up. They were part of *her* life. The photographs depicted members of *her* family. They belonged to her as much as they did to me.

"Here," I said, handing her the photographs. "I'm sorry. I wasn't thinking."

She took them back into the house.

Time passed, the seasons ebbed and flowed, the pages flew from the calendar. I received a bulky letter from my landlord with my lease renewal. I found it hard to believe that a year had elapsed. The brevity of life, a proposition I had dismissed when young as hopelessly banal and patently false, now seemed to be perhaps the one profound truth we all eventually confront. You did not have the opportunity to experiment with endless versions of yourself, to reinvent, to explore and retreat, to fail and start over.

That's not necessarily a disheartening discovery. It's a form of progress. The sense of limitation that overtakes you as you enter middle age forces you to sharpen your focus. Which was what I found I was doing. I also found after a while that the fog was lifting. I felt more alert, more energetic; my associative powers had improved; I had greater recall. Eventually, my daughter started wanting to sleep over again.

One night I came home from the gym and poured myself a scotch. The silence of the apartment had by then lost its desolate quality; at times it seemed almost serene. I called my daughter; she was jubilant over an A she had scored on a history test and a sleepover she had planned for the weekend. My wife got on the phone. She had received my check, and was enjoying the volunteer work she had begun. After I hung up the phone, I turned on the television. The Knicks were leading the Suns in the fourth quarter. It was an ordinary evening, but for some reason, as I settled down to watch the game that night, as one of the Knicks scored and I took a sip of scotch, I experienced a small but distinct, almost thrilling, stir of vindication. I knew this was dangerous to say, even to myself—that it tempted fate—but for the moment our lives seemed in order: we had done the right thing after all.

But that was just one night. There were other nights, nights when sitting down for a meal alone I would wonder if, as my wife prepared dinner, she caught herself listening for the sound of the front door opening, for me to come home after a day at the office. Late in the evening, unable to go to sleep, I would lie on the sofa with the lights out, playing music my wife had discovered, *Songs of the Auvergne* or *Tout les Matins du Monde,* on the stereo, and the memories of moments of my marriage—of the family we had been— would inhabit the room so completely that the walls disappeared. I would see the three of us. Running through the autumn leaves in the park, Jessica in the middle, wearing the hooded red parka we bought for her when she was four, holding me and my wife by the hand, pulling us after her in her eagerness. Clowning in sunglasses at the airport before a trip to London, pressing our heads together for the photograph I would take by holding the camera at arm's length. Shrieking with laughter at the way the new kitten, shut in the hallway, reached her paw beneath the kitchen door to swat at marbles my daughter rolled toward her. My daughter and I surprising my wife with the homeless man we once brought back to the house to share Thanksgiving dinner.

The three of us. It was always meant to be the three of us. This unshakable conviction would, on such evenings, leave me immobilized with grief. I thought I had escaped being punished for adultery. But this ache of regret, this bereavement, this sense that I had exiled myself forever from the two people on earth with whom I truly belonged—this was, I realized, the punishment. I became convinced on those nights that I had lost not just my wife and daughter but the best of myself, that I had willfully turned away from what was intended to be the central experience of my life.

But those nights passed as well.

For a long time after I left my wife I continued to wear my wedding ring. I felt about it the way I had the first time I had moved out, into the one-room apartment with the view of the dogwood and the moss-stained brick wall. The ring was familiar, comforting, a small weight I had become accustomed to carrying. Its presence on my finger declared to me that I had taken the idea of my marriage seriously, that I was still committed, if not to the marriage itself, to the responsibilities it entailed, to my wife and my daughter. Other people did not understand this sentiment. "Why are you still wearing your ring?" Alex had asked me the night we'd had dinner. "You're separated, aren't you?" The question had irritated me at the time. Why were these women so obsessed with the symbolism of this minor piece of jewelry? I wondered. It was a trinket, a bauble, an irrelevance. But I wasn't being honest with myself. After all, Alex did have a point. Why *was* I still wearing it? I had asked myself the next day. Did it mean I was clinging to a version of myself that no longer fit the facts? Did it mean I was afraid of something?

I started taking off the ring temporarily, tugging it gingerly over my knuckle, which was swollen from a racquetball injury. At first I kept the ring in my pocket along with my change and keys and subway tokens. My finger was aware of its absence and I often slipped it back on. But I did that less and less, and one morning, collecting my change from the platter where I kept it overnight, I left the ring there. But even after I stopped wearing the ring I saw it every morning when I filled my pockets—with the date of our wedding day engraved on the inner surface, it lay among the foreign coins and misplaced keys heaped on the platter, the various other fragments of shaped metal that once served a purpose in my life but now no longer did.

I enjoyed the sight of the ring. It engendered a sense of loss, but I had by then learned to live with such feelings, even to welcome them. They afforded me my only access to the past. I would pick up the ring, weigh it in my hand, polish it with my thumb. The ring made me realize how so many of the truths we discover come too late to do us any good, for it reminded me of how much there was that I had loved about my marriage, even when it no longer worked, and of how much I missed it, and would always miss it, my marriage and the vanished, unrecoverable family that my wife and my daughter and I had once formed.